The
Collected Poems of
ROY CAMPBELL
VOLUME 3

The
Collected Poems of
ROY CAMPBELL

VOLUME 3

[TRANSLATIONS]

with a Foreword by Edith Sitwell

THE BODLEY HEAD
LONDON

Roy Campbell's translations of
Horace's *The Art of Poetry*, three poems by Rafael Morales,
and two poems by J. Paço d'Arcos
© Mary Campbell 1960

Foreword © Edith Sitwell 1960
Printed in Great Britain for
THE BODLEY HEAD LTD
10 Earlham Street, London w.c.2
by William Clowes and Sons Ltd,
London and Beccles
Set in Monotype Centaur
First published 1960

FOREWORD

by Edith Sitwell

Roy Campbell was one of the very few great poets of our time.

For this reason I shall discuss not only his translations (poems that flowered as much from his blood as from the blood of the original poets) but also the poems in which he had no collaborator.

The flower of all his poems—original and translated—sprang from his blood; each was rooted there.

In *Appendices to a Poet in New York*[1] Federico García Lorca is quoted as saying, in a lecture: "Manuel Torres, to my mind a man of exemplary blood-culture, once uttered this splendid phrase, while listening to Falla playing his *Nocturno del Generalife*: 'Whatever has black sounds, has *duende*[2]' . . . These 'black sounds' are the mystery, the roots that probe through the mire that we all know of, and do not understand, but which furnishes us with whatever is sustaining in art."

The mire, perhaps, is only another word, in this case, for the blood.

Roy Campbell had this *"duende"*.

His original poems are of a great stature, and have a giant's strength and power of movement, without a giant's heaviness. In the Sacred Books of China (The Li Ki, translated by James Legge: Book XVII: Section II, Yo Ki) there is this sentence: "The ancient kings brought it [music] into harmony with the energy that produces life." That might have been said of Mr. Campbell's vital rhythms.

The poems have, too, an extraordinary sensuous beauty—a sensuousness that is extremely rare in our time.

Everything, even the humblest flower, is transformed into greatness:

> "Where jasmine clings like thunder to the peaks,
> Or makes a dewy starlight with its shade
> Where through the noon the gloaming is delayed."
> (*Flowering Rifle*: Book V. *Collected Poems*, Vol. II.)

[1] Translated by Ben Belet: Thames and Hudson.
[2] *duende*: inspiration, magic.

5

Some of his works were, to quote the words of one of Porphyry's *Oracles*, "Pure fire compressed into holy forms". Others have the vigour of a rushing wind, or have the strong and lovely movement of

"Horses, young horses, and the waves of the sea."

(I do not know who wrote that lovely phrase—I know only that it is a translation from the Greek.)

Campbell had an extraordinary and flawless technique, with every variety, from the superb strength and savagery of *Mazeppa* to the exquisite, cool, vital, dancing sound of *The Palm* (*Collected Poems*, Vol. I)—a sound which seems, actually, to reproduce that of air moving among leaves—and to the beauty, the ineffable sound, that is like that of water lapping, of the translation from St. John of the Cross, *Upon a Gloomy Night*, which is, perhaps, the chief glory of this present book.

His use of rhyme is masterly.

"The profit of rhyme," said Whitman, in the Preface to *Leaves of Grass*, "is that it drops seeds of a sweeter and more luxuriant thyme; and of uniformity that it conveys itself into its own roots in the ground out of sight. The rhyme and the uniformity of perfect forms show the free growth of metrical laws, and bud from them as unerringly and loosely as lilacs or roses on a bush, and take shapes as compact as the shapes of chestnuts and oranges and melons and pears, and shed the perfume impalpable to form."

That "perfume impalpable to form" was shed by all Roy Campbell's rhymed poems.

He could, and did, write superb sonnets—such as that to Camões (published in his book *Portugal*: Max Reinhardt), which ends thus:

" . . . yet of his sorrows king
He shouldered high his voluntary Cross,
Wrestled his hardships into forms of beauty,
And taught his gorgon destinies to sing."

Those lines might have been addressed to himself—whose gorgon destinies, however, were averted from turning his heart to stone by his deeply beloved wife.

The greatest triumph of this present book is the ineffable translation from St. John of the Cross, *Upon a Gloomy Night*, to which I have referred already, and which is certainly among the great poems of our time. It is almost equalled by another translation, *Coplas about the soul which suffers with impatience to see God*:

> "I live without inhabiting
> Myself, in such a wise that I
> Am dying that I do not die."

The other principal beauties of this book are Quevedo's *On Lisi's Golden Hair* and *On a White Foal dying on a Moonlit Night*, after Rafael Morales. These are the greatest triumphs, but they are almost rivalled by Baudelaire's *Ill Luck*—a wonderful transcription this—*The Albatross*, in which one senses the vast sweep of those great wings, and his *The Giantess*.

But the whole book is full of wonders, and all have the genius—to quote from Lorca once more—"not only of form, but the marrow of form".

CONTENTS

9

PART SIX
From Baudelaire's Les Fleurs du Mal

PART SEVEN
Portuguese Poems

PREFACE

The first poems my husband translated, when he was eighteen years old, were from Rimbaud and Baudelaire, and he continued translating all through his life. He translated nearly all the works of García Lorca and, in a few months while at the B.B.C., the whole of Baudelaire. He did the whole of St. John of the Cross, and many complete plays by the greater dramatists of the Golden Age of Spanish Literature (Lope de Vega, Calderón de la Barca, Tirso, Cervantes), besides a large number of single poems by Góngora, Quevedo and many modern poets. At the time of his death he was compiling an anthology of Portuguese poets, and had already translated many poems from the time of Gil Vicente to the present day. The poems in this volume are a small, and, it is hoped, representative, selection from this large collection of translations; Horace's *Art of Poetry* and several shorter poems are here published for the first time. *Upon a Gloomy Night* (St. John of the Cross), which was included in *Collected Poems, Vol. I*, takes its place naturally in a collection of outstanding translations, and is thus reprinted here. *Counsel* (Manuel Bandeira) was wrongly included in *Collected Poems, Vol. II*, as an original poem, and appears correctly here as a translation.

The translations of the poems of Federico García Lorca are published with permission of his heirs, All Rights Reserved. The translations from *Poems of St. John of the Cross* and *Poems of Baudelaire: Les Fleurs du Mal* are reprinted by permission of the Harvill Press.

I should also like to thank Dame Edith Sitwell for her Foreword, full of such beautiful things, and only one among her many tributes both spoken and written to my husband since his death.

MARY CAMPBELL

PART ONE

Four French Poems

The Bee—Paul Valéry

However sharp and dire you shoot
Your dart, O golden bee, I place
Only the flimsiest veil of lace
Over my frail of tender fruit.

Sting on the breast this gourd so fresh
Where love, in death or sleep, lies leaden;
So may some inkling of me redden
The rounded and rebellious flesh.

I need quick pain, a prompt alert:
Far better than a lingering hurt
The keenest pang that soonest flies.

Gold spar, light up the sense you pierce,
Infinitesimal yet fierce,
Without whose sting love sleeps or dies.

★

Drunken Boat—Arthur Rimbaud

I felt no more the guidance of my tow-men
As I came down by listless river-coasts.
To serve for targets, whooping Redskin bowmen
Had pinned them naked to their coloured posts.

Bearer of Flemish corn or English cotton,
I cared no more for crews of any kind.
When with my own the scuffle was forgotten,
The rivers let me rove as I inclined.

Into the furious chopping of the tides
Last winter, heedless as a child, I glided;
Nor have the unmoored headlands on their sides
Sustained so proud a buffeting as I did.

The Storm has blessed my watches in the spray:
Cork-light I danced the waves for ten whole nights
(Those everlasting maulers of their prey!)
Nor missed the foolish blink of harbour-lights.

Sweet, as to children the tart flesh of apples,
Green water pierced my shell with juicy shudder,
Spewing a wine of azure blots and dapples
That rinsed me round, dispersing helm and rudder.

Since then I have gone bathing in the hymn
Of a sea sprayed with stars and whitely creaming:
Devouring the green depths where, flotsam dim,
Sometimes a drowning man descends half-dreaming:

Where with slow-pulsing and delirious fires,
To flush the blue, while day blazed white above,
Stronger than wine and vaster than your lyres,
Ferments the crimson bitterness of love.

I've known the surf, the waterspouts, the tide:
Lightning-split skies: the dusk: the dawn upheld
Like a whole swarm of doves; and I have spied
Sometimes, what Man believes he has beheld.

Lighting long wisps in violent panoramas,
I have seen mystic horrors scrawl the sun:
Far waves, like actors in the ancient dramas,
Unroll their flickering shutters as they run.

I've dreamed the green night lit with dazzling frost
A kiss that to the sea's eyes slowly grew,
The flow of saps to human knowledge lost,
And singing phosphorescence gold and blue.

Like mad stampedes of cattle on the prairies,
With breakers I have charged the reefs and screes
For months: nor dreamed the lit feet of the Maries
Could force a snaffle of those snorting seas.

Blurring with flowers the eyes of human leopards,
I've whirled Floridas none yet set eyes on,
Where, stretching coloured reins, the Iris shepherds
Her glaucous flocks beneath the sea's horizon.

I've seen the swamps ferment, huge creels of rushes,
Where rots a whole Leviathan as it sleeps,
Amidst dead calms collapsing water-gushes,
And distances cascading to the deeps:

Glaciers, white suns, pearl waves, skies of red coals:
At limits of brown gulfs, foul objects stranded:
Where huge bug-eaten snakes from twisted boles
Fell dying with black perfumes where they landed.

I would have shown those bream of the blue billow
To children, those gold fish, those fish that sing;
Foam flowers for my escape have smoothed a pillow
And winds ineffable have waved my wing.

Tired martyr, round the poles and tropics rolled,
The wave, whose sobs my cradle rocked at ease,
Raised flowers of shade with spiracles of gold
And left me like a woman on her knees.

Half-island, tilting at my sides the frays
And tail-shots of the blond-eyed birds that scream,
I wandered, while across my flimsy stays
Drowned men descended backwards down to dream.

Lost in the hair of coves or like a shaft
Shot into birdless ether, I, lost boat,
Whose sea-drunk corpse no Hanseatic craft
Nor monitor could salvage or refloat,

Free, smoking, by the violet fog embraced,
Have broached the sky's red wall and bored it through,
Which bears, so dainty to good poets' taste,
Lichens of sun, and mucus of the blue.

Scribbled with small electric moons, mad plank,
With black sea-horses harnessed to my gunnels,
I've run, while Summer bashed to dust, and sank
The jet-blue sky to swirl down blazing funnels,

I who have quaked to hear, at fifty leagues,
The rut of Behemoths and Maelstroms roar,
Threader of endless calms whom naught fatigues,
Am sick for Europe's towers of ancient lore.

Starred archipelagoes I've seen and islands
Where maddening skies, to tempt the rover, flower,
Where hide you in those nights of topless silence
(Millions of golden birds!) predestined Power?

But, true, I've wept too much. The dawns are fearful.
Each moon is loathsome. Suns are sour to me.
Salt love has bloated me and sogged me tearful.
May my keel splinter! Give me to the sea!

If there's a northern water that I crave,
It's the black slush, at scented close of day,
Whereon a child releases, sadly grave,
A boat frail as the butterflies of May.

No more, bathed in your languor, waves! I'll trim
Her seawake where the cotton-clipper flies:
Nor cross the pomp of flags and flames: nor swim
Beneath the convict-hulks' resentful eyes.

★

Bestiary—Guillaume Apollinaire

ORPHEUS
    That signal verge of power! Let it be noted.
That majesty of line! What could be grander?
It is the voice of light made sound, as quoted
By Hermes Trismegistus in 'Poimander'.

20

THE HORSE   My hard and formal dreams will break and
                         ride you,
                         Your proud fate in the golden car be mine,
                         My verses, frenzy-stretched, be reins to guide
                         you,
                         A paragon of song in every line.

THE GOAT   The shaggy fleece this she-goat wears
                         And that which so much hardship costs
                         To Jason—are not worth two hairs
                         Of that to which my heart is lost.

THE SNAKE   You rage at beauty: and I grieve
                         To think what lovely victims bore
                         Your lust to murder or deceive.
                         Egypt, Eurydice and Eve—
                         And I could name a couple more.

THE CAT   Grant me a hole in which to live,
                         A wife with sense, to share my home,
                         A cat among my books to roam—
                         Such friends for every season, give!
                         For want of whom I cannot live.

THE DROMEDARY With his four dromedaries Don
                         Pedro d'Alfaroubeira's gone
                         To view the world, as I would do
                         Had I four dromedaries too.

THE MOUSE   Fine days, O mice of time, how dearly
                         Your nibbling stealth my life must pay
                         Twenty eight years I've reached, or nearly—
                         Mostly ill-lived, or chucked away.

THE ELEPHANT   As elephants their ivory wear
                         My riches in my mouth I bear.
                         O purple death! . . . I buy renown
                         With melodies of verb and noun.

| THE PRAWN | Incertitude, divinely dear!
| | You and myself to get from here
| | Must shunt, as prawns do, face to rear,
| | Reversing gear, reversing gear.

THE PRAWN Incertitude, divinely dear!
You and myself to get from here
Must shunt, as prawns do, face to rear,
Reversing gear, reversing gear.

THE SIRENS Dear Sirens, under what sad maledictions
Far out to sea at midnight flow your tears?
I too, Oh Sea, am thronged with vocal fictions.
My singing ships go by the name of years.

ORPHEUS Bait with your heat: through heaven troll
your line.
O Fisherman! What fish has yet sufficed,
In form or taste, to vie with the divine
Sweet fish, that is my Saviour, JESUS
CHRIST.

★

Sorrow of a Star—Guillaume Apollinaire

A fine Minerva of my head was daughter,
A star of blood forever marks the place
(Heaven above, and reason at the base)
Where long she had been arming for the slaughter.

That's why of all the griefs with which I'm ridden
This starred, nigh-fatal wound is not my worst.
I have a secret evil more accurst
Than any other soul has ever hidden.

And so I burn, with anguish for my pyre,
As glow-worms panting in their own hot sheen;
As in one soldier's heart all France is seen,
Or lily's heart—its pollen-scented fire.

★

22

PART TWO

Horace—The Art of Poetry

Horace: Ars Poetica

THE ART OF POETRY
(Dedicated to the Pisos, the Father and his Two Sons)

Say, were a painter to a horse's neck
To fit a human head, then fledge and fleck
With motley plumes strange limbs picked up at random,
Hitching a fine girl's body in a tandem
To a foul fish, for its posterior half—
At such a sight could you forbear to laugh?
A written book would prove as strange a fright
Believe me, my dear Pisos, as the sight
Of such a picture, were it fashioned so,
And, like a sick man's dream, so mixed, that no
Headpiece or foot could fit to any single
Whole form, but all chaotically mingle.
You say that painters with us poets share
An equal right to chance things, and to dare.
We know it. All the license that we claim
We grant to them: but not to mate what's tame
With what is fierce, to marry snakes with birds,
Or roaring tigers to the bleating herds.

Some works prance forth and promise in their stride,
Patched with fine purple, to shine far and wide
With grand beginnings—on Diana's grove
And altar: on "the mazy streams that rove[1]
Through lush fields": on the rainbow, or the Rhine
Painted descriptively in words as fine.
Such works are for another time, not now.
To paint a cypress one may well know how,
But what if one's commissioned, for one's cheque,
To paint a sailor swimming from a wreck[2]

[1] Apparently in this passage he is referring to, or quoting from, well known contemporary poems, now lost.

[2] Such works were commonly commissioned as ex-votos to hang in temples, by sailors who had escaped from wrecks. The practice continues today in Italy, Spain and Portugal.

That's battered by the waves beyond repair,
While hope seems lost, and life is in despair?
What was to be a wine jar will be found
A milk jug when the potter's wheel goes round.
In short, whatever work you undertake,
Simple and uniform be what you make.

Father, and both sons worthy such a sire!
Semblance is what we poets most admire.
Affecting briefness—I obscurely darkle:
Or smoothness—then I lose all verve and sparkle:
One bard grows turgid when he would seem grand:
One, fearing thunder, crawls along the sand:
One who attempts too lavishly to vary
A single subject, if he is not wary,
Will make wild boars the natives of the seas
Or populate with porpoises the trees.
If to shun dangers we too wildly start,
We'll meet disaster, if we lack true art.
Near the Aemilian school, far down the Row,
There is a certain sculptor that I know,
Who moulds bronze well when doing hair or nails,
But it's with the whole body that he fails.
Now, when I want to write, I would no more
Wish to resemble him, than if I wore
My nose turned sideways, though folk thought me fine
For my black eyes and raven locks ashine.
Oh, choose a subject equal to your strength,
You poets! And consider at great length
What load your back and shoulders must refuse
And what is best adapted to your thews.
Choose but a subject well within your border
And you'll enjoy the clearness born of order:
The language will reward you with abundance
And you'll escape confusion and redundance.
If I err not, this is the grace of measure
And constitutes its excellence and pleasure—
That every thing be said at the right second,
Cancelling anything that might be reckoned

26

Unfit for present use, or storing it
For apter time and place, as should befit
One who attempts a poem. With due care
And taste, you'll win success; you might prepare
Some pretext to renew a well-worn word
With sound and meaning until then unheard.
Then, if perhaps some new ice must be broken
To speak abstruse new things, till now unspoken,
You'll get a splendid chance new words to coin
Unknown to Romans of the kilted loin.[1]
New words, if they're not overdone too far,
Will be accepted, if you fill your jar,
Sparingly always, from a Grecian fount.
Yet why can Plautus or Caecilius count
On Romans for the very full amount
Of license, which to Virgil and to Varius
They now deny? My small due, though precarious,
Why should they grudge? since in the ancient tongue
Of Ennius and of Cato new terms sprung
To life. It always was, and will be, licit
That new terms for new things should be implicit,
And that new coinage should be stamped, and printed,
And dated with the year when it was minted.
As forests change their leaves at each year's end
The earliest leaves to sprout the first descend—
So it's with words: down falls the race outworn:
And like the young of human-kind, new-born,
The young words thrive and bloom. Ourselves and all
Things that are ours to death at length must fall.
We can lead Neptune far inland to shelter
Our fleets from Boreas and his stormy welter,
Or (truly royal labour!) we can dry
Marshes, where once the oars of boats were plied
But whence the neighbouring towns are now supplied
From labours of the plough: or make a river
Change course, the sprouting cornfields to deliver
Which once it flooded, but now learns the ways
To better things. Yet mortal works decay.

[1] The ancient Romans wore loin cloths, not togas as in Horace's time.

27

Still less can last the fleeting grace of speech:
Many old words, now fallen out of reach,
May be revived, and those in favour now,
If Usage wills, may wither on the bough,
For in her judgement lies the fate of all
Live speech, and by its words must stand or fall.

How deeds of Kings and Captains, and the woes
Of warfare can be sung—great Homer shows.
To distiches, the dirges of despair
Were yoked at first, and thanks for granted prayer.
Who first invented elegy, the court
Must yet decide. With his iambics (short
And long) rage armed Archilochus to smite.
Both comic sock and buskin tall unite
To find it suited to alternate talk,
And apt the cat-calls of the pit to baulk.
It fits with action too. Her lyre to grace,
The Muse reserved the Gods and all their race,
The jockey and the horse who win first place,
The champion pugilist, the loves of youth,
And praise of wine that loosens tongues with truth.
To call me poet, it would be most strange
Did I not know each sympton, beat, or change
In the verse-metres. Should I, through false shame,
Choose ignorance, rather than learned fame?

A subject fit for Comedy rebels
Against the Tragic metre. He who tells
Thyestes' tale the theme must never mock
With common speech, that suits the comic sock.
Let each theme keep the tone that is decreed.
Yet there are times when Comedy has need
Of lofty tones, as when loud Chremes storms
In swollen tones; and so the tragic norms
May vary too, as when in common prose
Peleus and Telephus recount their woes
In exiled poverty: they must discard
The thundering bombast that they spout so hard,

And in plain simple language play their part
In order thus to reach the hearer's heart.

Mere form is not enough: grace too must thrill
And lead the hearer's spirit where it will.
As most men's faces smile on those who smile,
So, too, they answer those who weep the while.
If you wish me to grieve, then you grieve first.
So, Telephus, the woes with which you're curst
Will pierce me too: but if your words suit ill,
I'll slumber on the bench, or laugh my fill.
Sad tones best suit a face expressing sorrow:
Blustering tones an angry frown should borrow:
Quips for the merry: stern words for the grave
Thus nature shapes the ways that we behave.
In meeting every change of fate she brings
Joy, or enrages us, or downward flings
And tortures us beneath a load of grief—
And then in word she makes us find relief.
If with the actor's fate his words don't fit
Guffaws will rise both from the stalls and pit.
Vast differences in their speech divide
A hero and a god: a gulf as wide
Severs a nursemaid, and a noble dame:
An old man, and a youth whose heart's aflame:
A pedlar, from a tiller of the glebe: an
Assyrian, or an Argive, from a Theban.

Follow tradition or, if you invent,
Be self-consistent. If you would present
Achilles being honoured, on the stage,
Let him be reckless, ruthless, full of rage:
Let him proclaim there are no laws for him,
Appealing to his arms with gestures grim.
Fierce let Medea be, Ixion—foresworn,
Io—a wanderer: let Orestes mourn.
If it's an untried subject you explore
With some new personage not staged before,
Let him keep constant from the first to last,
And faithful to the mould where he was cast.

To treat of humdrum things in one's own way
Is hard. And it is better, in a play,
To weave the tale of Troy into your act
Than broach an untried subject, still intact.
On public ground you will win private rights
If you don't loiter when the path invites.
Nor as a base translator word for word
Follow your model as a sheep the herd;
And if you leap not in that narrow well
In which the billygoat of Aesop fell,
From whence for shame you never can depart
Bound by the rules of imitative art.
With such a line your poem should not start
As did the Cyclic poet's of old time—
"Of Priam's fate and famous wars I'll rhyme."
What could this braggard give us to fulfil
His promise? So might labour some huge hill,
Struggle in agonising throes, and, after,
Bring forth a mouse deserving of our laughter.
Better by far he is who makes no fuss
Nor strains himself, but starts his poem thus:
"Sing, Muse, about the man, who, when Troy fell,
Saw the world's customs and its towns as well."
He does not wish to bring us smoke from fire,
But to bring light from smoke is his desire.
So that his wondrous tales may shine the best—
Of Scylla, and the Cyclops, and the rest.
Nor does he start, with Meleager's death,
Great Diomed's return: nor waste his breath
To start the siege of Troy from the twin eggs.
He rushes on, despising lees and dregs,
And hustles us towards the story's middle.
With what he can't make grand, he does not fiddle:
So cunningly does he create, so mingle
His myths and facts that in the end a single
Constancy's won—beginning, middle, ending
All in one whole harmoniously blending.

The public both expect this, and I, too,
(If sympathetic hearers you would woo,

Who'll wait the curtain and forbear to rise
Till "Give me my applause", the singer cries)—
That you should heed the manners of each age
And suit their shifting tempers to the stage.
The child, who now can speak and walk upright,
In sporting with his playmates takes delight,
Easily flies into a rage, once in it,
Lays it aside, and changes every minute.
The beardless youth, when from his tutor freed,
Will find his chief delight in hound and steed,
And on the grassy Campus loves to roll.
As soft as wax to vice, his peevish soul
Refuses all sage counsel and control
Feckless, a spendthrift, seized with quick desires,
But quick to change them as his fancy tires.
With manhood both his character and taste
Are changed: he seeks by friends to be embraced,
And to earn wealth. A slave, now, to ambitions,
He fears the outcome of his own decisions.
An old man by great evils is beset;
Losing both health and sleep his wealth to get,
He fears to touch it, or to spend his cash.
In his affairs he lacks all fire and dash,
Procrastinates, is sparing in his hopes,
Sluggish, and dull; yet greedily he gropes
For longer life: grumbling, with surly tongue,
Praising the good old days when he was young,
And cursing modern youth. The years may bring
Many great blessings. Many too take wing
When they recede. So, lest we should assign
To youth the part of age, or else combine
The part of youth with manhood, let us pause
To study every age, its traits and flaws.

Deeds on the stage can either be recited
Or acted. People's minds are less excited
By things which penetrate them through the ear
Than things that to the truthful eye appear,
And what by the spectator can be seen.
Yet you must never put upon the scene

What could be done off-stage: you must not show
Anything that the audience cannot know
Through witnesses' accounts. Let not Medea
Publicly kill her sons, but in idea;
Nor impious Atreus cook his human steak,
Nor Procne turn a bird, Cadmus a snake,
In public. Were you such a trick to try,
Incredulously I would scorn the lie!

More acts, or less, than five no play should count
If it's to be encored. Let no God mount
The stage unless the knot he has to free
Is worthy the deliverer. Let there be
In conversation never more than three.

The Chorus should sustain his manly part
And function: nor between the acts depart
In what he sings from that which to his plot
Fully pertains—discarding what does not.
Siding with good, he should give counsel well,
And as a friend, striving all wrath to quell.
Encouraging the just, praising sobriety
And homely fare, with peace, and law, and piety,
He should keep secrets, and devoutly pray
Good fortune from the proud be turned away
To the unlucky persons in the play.

The wooden flute (now turned a brazen strumpet
Bound up in brass, the rival of the trumpet)
Once led the pristine chorus with its song
For seats as yet pressed by a lighter throng—
Chaste modest people, sober people, too,
Who could be counted since they were so few:

But since our victor race spread through the Earth,
And walls around its cities swelled in girth,
And since it was no longer held a crime
To pledge one's Genius in the festal time
And drink by daylight—rhythm, tune, and measure
Acquired more license, liberty, and leisure.

What good taste could be hoped for from a crowd
Which mixes boors with burghers, poor with proud,
And some still sweating from the fields they ploughed?
Since then, to the old art the flautist added
Display and pomp, as to and fro he gadded
From wing to wing, parading up and down
The sumptuous train of his pretentious gown,
Flaunting his finery, and nimbly prancing
To supplement his music with his dancing.
So, also, to the plain old fashioned lyre
Were added extra strings of twangling wire
A strange, audacious diction to inspire:
The chorus then began to utter grave
Good counsels, or with prophecies to rave
Like those of Delphi's priestess in her cave.

The bard who first in Tragedy[1] competed
For a mere paltry billygoat that bleated,
Brought naked satyrs on the stage who cracked
Lewd jests, but left the gravity intact,
For the spectators had observed the rite
Of copious libations and were tight,
And lawlessly inclined. Thus it was needful
With quips and novelties to keep them heedful.
So it behoved the poet to seek favour
Through these coarse satyrs and their goatish savour,
Before he passed to other subjects, graver.
But while we graft our jests to graver thought,
No god nor hero ever should be caught,
Redhanded, in some lowdown tavern-hovel
Using the vulgar tongue, with words that grovel.
Yet, shunning baseness, do not let your speech
Spurn the firm earth, for empty clouds to reach.
True Tragedy, scorning to speak what's trivial,
(Like a proud matron forced, on the convivial
Occasion of a holy day, to dance)
Amongst the frisking satyrs looks askance.

[1] Tragedy gets its name from the goat that was given as a prize to
the winner of the earliest Olympic contests between poets. It means
"goat-poetry", from *tragos* (a goat) and *aeidō* (to sing or recite).

My Piso friends, true Tragedy to write,
I'll use no trivial words my theme to slight,
Nor of what's tragic so far lose the sight
That it's no matter whether Davus speak
With Pythias, the vile and shameless Greek,
Who, cheating Simo, earned a tidy wad,
Or with Silenus, guardian of the god.
My aim is song, drawn from what's so familiar
That all who think it easy, will prove sillier,
In the attempt, than they expect. When much
Sweat has been spent, they'll fail the magic touch.
Such is the power of making terms cohere,
That beauty from the commonplace, by sheer
Sense of arrangement, shines out bright and clear.

Fauns, from the forest brought, may well beware
Of acting as if on the Public Square,
Or aping precious dandies of the city,
Or cracking jokes more crapulous than witty,
Since Roman Knights and Freemen scorn such scenes
As please the eaters of the nuts and beans.[1]
That beat, wherein a short precedes a long
Syllable's what we call Iambic song,
Which means "fleet-footed". It is so much fleeter
Than sense, that we miscall it the "three-metre",
The whole line's sum perfected in their halves;
Whole legs find alibis in thighs and calves;
"Three-beats" we call it, though its beats are six,
And roll on evenly, and do not mix.
Not long ago, to give it poise and weight,
Iambus took the Spondee in its gait,
But never in the fourth foot or the second
Of the Iambus is the Spondee reckoned.
In the trimetres Accius wrote—it's rare:
And in what Ennius, without skill or care,
Unloaded on the stage—you'll find it there,
Either that in revising he'd no part,
Or that he was too ignorant of art.

[1] Those who occupied the cheap seats regaled themselves with roasted
beans and chestnuts.

Not every critic spots the faulty fool,
So undeserved indulgence is the rule.
But if I then stampede and jump the fence,
To a safe pardon can I make pretence?
At best, I'll have escaped without due blame,
And yet can make no bid for learned fame.
For you, Greek models are the best to handle
Whether by day, or by the midnight candle.
And yet you say 'twas our forbears who taught us
To praise the metres and the wit of Plautus . . .
Too tolerant they were—too kindly foolish
Mistaking for true wit what's coarse and mulish,
Since we by ear and finger can sort out
What's clumsy from what's right, beyond all doubt.

Thespis, they say, discovered first the Muse
Of tragedy, before her name made news.
He used to cart his plays around in wagons
Acted by clowns stained with the lees of flagons.
Aeschylus, later, improvised the planks,
Tall buskins, robes, the players' masks, and (thanks
To him) the stately gait and lofty strain
That till his time no drama could attain.
To this succeeded the old Comedy.
It won some honour, but was far too free;
Licentious to excess, it was thereafter
Checked by the law, for its injurious laughter.
The law was passed. The chorus then became
Harmlessly dumb, to its enduring shame.

Our own bards tried all styles, nor has less glory
Been won, when keeping to their native story
(Whether in tragic or in comic vein),
They cease to follow in the Grecian train.
If all our poets polished up their style
And had the patience both to pare and file,
Then Latin might have shone supreme in verse
As in armed glory, through the universe.

You then, of Numa's stock,[1] should ban all lines
Which the bard neither alters nor refines,
With many a blot, through many a lengthy day,
And polishes and files the best he may,
Till manicured and burnished twenty times,
A well cut nail may test and prove his rhymes.

Because Democritus says native wit
Is greater then mere art, and won't admit
Some bards to Helicon—some sprout long hair
With shaggy beards, and nails they never pare.
Shunning mankind they stray in lonely paths
And shun alike the barbers and the baths.
Thinking to join the poets' deathless ranks
If from Licinus'[2] shears he saves the hanks
Of a shag pate, that not all the hellebore
Of all three Anticyras[3] could restore.
How daft of me to purge myself of bile
Whenever lusty Spring begins to smile!
None could sing better, but it's not worth while,
I'll be the whetstone that can sharpen steel:
Although it cannot cut, I shall reveal
The poet's duties and his task: and whence
He draws his ammunition and his rations;
What nourishes him best, I'll show: what fashions
His talent: what befits him best and what
Doesn't: which course to follow, and which not.

Of all good writing wisdom is the fount.
The wise Socratic pages can recount
Your subject. When you have the theme, the words
Will follow it along in flocks and herds.
Learn what you owe your country and your friend
What love upon a parent should attend,

[1] The Pisos were aristocrats claiming descent from Numa Pompilius
and related to Julius Caesar's wife Calpurnia.

[2] Apparently a fashionable hairdresser in Rome.

[3] Hellebore was supposed to be a cure for lunacy. The Anticyras
were cities of the same name situated on a mountain range north of
Corinth, where hellebore grew in great abundance. Hellebore is also a
purge for bile.

A guest, or brother. Learn what is expected
Of senator or judge: how war's directed
By a supreme commander in the field—
That each in his true role may be revealed.
He, who in imitative skill rejoices,
From life and manners should take living voices.
Though fashioned without grace or strength, a play
Is far more pleasing if it can display
Characters drawn to life, and has some witty
Patches of dialogue—than all the pretty,
Far-better-written verse that's void of thought,
And sounding bombast signifying naught.

The Muse gave native wit to Grecian folk:
With a rotundity of style they spoke
Lusting for fame. But we in long division,
Addition, and subtraction, learn precision,
And how to split the As[1] up into parts.
For sums and figures, we neglect the arts.
The Master says "Now, you, Albinus' son,
Answer. If from five-twelfths the weight of one
Ounce is subtracted, what have we got left?"
"A third." "Good! in your Business you'll be deft.
And if I add an ounce, what then?" "A half."
When this base passion for the Golden Calf,
This eating rust, has fouled the Roman mind,
What poetry can we expect to find
Worthy with oil of cedar to be swept
Or within boards of cypress to be kept?
Poets wish either to instruct or please
Or both at once. But do it by degrees,
And do it briefly, if you would instruct,
So that the mind retains the fruit it plucked.
One word too much will overflow and spill
After the brimming mind has had its fill,
From fancied fictions most delight is won
When nearest to reality they run.

[1] As is a Roman bronze coin, originally weighing about a pound,
reduced finally to half an ounce.

In plays be circumspect with the unreal
Nor from the Lamia let her human meal
Be saved out of her guts—a living child.
Plays without moral purpose are exiled
From the stage by our elders. Men of race
And breeding scorn a poem without grace.
You'll win, if you mix benefit with pleasure
Teaching and charming in an equal measure.
Such is the volume by the sale of which
Publishers like the *Soscii* grow rich.
Such is the book that makes the author's name
Cross seas and centuries with lasting fame.

Yet there are errors which we can forgive
Gladly. A harpstring will not always give
The note that hand and heart wished from the harp,
And for a flat note sometimes gives a sharp.
Nor will a bow hit whatsoever prey
It aims at. But when beauties oversway
The blemishes that carelessness let fall,
Or that our nature can't prevent at all,
I will not ban such poetry. What then?
A clerk who, making copies with his pen,
Though often warned, continues still to make,
In spite of everything, the same mistake,
Merits no mercy. So the zither-twanger
Who on the selfsame string bungles with clangour
Repeatedly, is laughed at. Thus I class
The poet who so blunders, as an ass,
With Choerilus, in whom a few good lines
The more provoke our laughter, when he shines.
I grieve when Homer nods: but every song
Is liable to tedium, if long.

A poem, like a picture, may appear
Better, far off: or better, standing near.
One woos the shade: another woos the light
And challenges the critic's piercing sight.
One having pleased us once, we can admire
No more: yet of another cannot tire.

You, elder son, though wise yourself and taught
By a wise father to judicious thought,
Mark well my words (in this I am no joker)
Only in some fields can the mediocre
Be suffered. Lawyers of a middling sort
Though of the great Messala falling short,
And knowing less than Aulus, have their use,
But for a middling poet? No excuse!
Nor Gods, nor men, nor publishers permit,
Even in their wildest dreams, the thought of it!
As at a pleasant feast we take offence
At a band out of tune, unguent too dense,
Or, in Sardinian honey, poppy seed—
Since of the like the banquet had no need—
So poems, written for the souls' delight;
If they should fail to reach the sheerest height,
Fall headlong down. The man who's weak at sport
Will never to the playing field resort:
If he's bad as a bowler and a quoiter
Around the Campus he's ashamed to loiter
For dread of people's laughter and contempt.
Yet those who can't write verses still attempt
To do so, and with neither dread nor shame
Insist on interfering in the game.
Why not? He's a free man perhaps free-born
With a knight's fortune—so he's safe from scorn.

But you, my friend, will not presume to slight
Minerva's will—your judgement is so right,
So sound your sense. But if you should be tempted
To rhyme, show first the work you have attempted
To some strict Maecius: after that, deposit
The script for nine years in your father's closet.
Unpublished work, one can delete or burn.
The voice, sent forth, can nevermore return.

When men lived in the wilds, Orpheus, the prophet,
Saw their bloodthirsty life, and warned them off it,
For doing which he won the mythic fame
Of making lions and fierce tigers tame:

And of Amphion's building Thebes they tell
Like tales. His lyre moved boulders with its spell,
And led them where he wanted them as well.
Of old it was thought wise to draw a line
'Twixt private things and public: to define
The sacred from the vulgar: to keep strict
The marriage law: loose love to interdict.
To build towns, and carve laws on slabs of wood
In those old times it was considered good.
And so on poets fame and glory fell,
And deified them, and their songs as well.
Then Homer won renown. Tyrtaeus drove
Men's souls, when in the Wars of Mars they strove.
Oracles spoke in song and showed the way
To better life. The poets in their day
Could sing preferment from the hearts of kings,
And after toil, in the Pierian springs,
Delight was found. So do not blush to follow
The lyre-skilled Muse and the divine Apollo.

Concerning a good poem, men enquire
Whether from art it stems, or native fire.
I find all effort vain which sets apart
Genius from toil, nature from conscious art.
For nature's talent needs the help of science
And vice versa—both in fond alliance.
He who would win the race before the rest
Must, even as a child, have stood the test
Of heat, cold, and fatigue. He must abstain
From Venus and from Bacchus. He who blows
The oboe at the Games learned what he knows
From a feared tutor by the dint of blows.
Not so verse-writers of the present day
"My verse is wonderful," is what they say,
"He who comes last be damned. I've but one shame
And that's to be surpassed: but all the same
I never learned a thing about the game."
Just like the public criers who collect
Crowds for some public sale which they expect,

The poet, if he owns a rich estate
Or leases property at a high rate,
Collects his flatterers, as meat does flies,
By flashing golden bribes before their eyes.
But if his power to such a pitch extends
That he to sumptuous feasts can treat his friends,
Or stand as surety for a poor man's debt,
Or rescue one whom law-suits have beset—
Confounding interests—he will never know
Whether his friends are hypocrites or no:
And you, yourself, if wishing to be pleasant,
You purpose giving anyone a present,
For heaven's sake, while he with joy is smitten,
Don't read him any verses you have written!
For he'll cry out "Fine! Wondrous! Perfect! Splendid!"
And beating time until the verse is ended
Grow pale, and weep with dewy eyes distended.
As you may see in funeral processions,
The hired mourners, more than the relations,
Whose grief is real, howl, rave, and tear their locks,
The flatterer, too, though in his heart he mocks,
More than the true admirer shows delight,
Rejoices, and applauds with all his might.

When monarchs wish true friendship to divine,
They put the person to the test of wine.
If you write verse, yet wish true friends to win,
Beware what lurks beneath the fox's skin.
When people read their verses to Quintilius,
His answer was straightforwardly punctilious—
"Mend this, I beg you. Then mend this": and when
You had tried vainly three or four times, then
He'd tell you to wipe everything away,
And start once more on what you had to say.
If you preferred your fluff to mending it,
He said no word: he did not mind a whit:
Without demur, he let you go your way
To be your own self-loving non-pareil.
A wise and honest judge will criticise
Limp verse in which no art or cunning lies:

Cancel what's harsh and rugged with a stroke:
Suppress pretentious bombast with a joke:
And make you light the gloom if you grow dark.
The necessary changes he'll remark—
In short he will become an Aristarch.
He will not say, "Why hurt a friend for trifles?"
Which later may be turned on him like rifles
And wound him mortally, when once the crowd
Jeers him to scorn, and hisses him aloud.

One fears and shuns the wretch with rabies bitten,
With jaundice or fanaticism smitten,
Or by Diana's wrath made lunatic;
So men shun crazy poets like Old Nick.
Children torment them, risking kicks and blows,
But high in air the poet rears his nose
And whinnies forth his verses as he goes.
If, one day, like a birdcatcher he fell,
Star-gazing after blackbirds, in a well—
And yelled "Help! Citizens!"—they'd let him yell!
To those who wished to save him, I would say
"Why, don't you know, he did himself away
On purpose and does not want any succours."
And then I'd tell the story to the suckers
Of the Sicilian bard—and how he died.
Empedocles wished to be deified
In people's minds, and so he leaped inside
Erupting Etna, with cool calculation.
Poets have rights to such self-immolation.
To rescue one against his will is wrong,
When he's committing suicide in song.
To rescue him's a crime. Such if you save—
He will not cease a famous death to crave,
Nor yet consent as human to behave.
It puzzles me how he conceived this passion
To scribble in so desperate a fashion.
What's certain is, he's mad, and, like a bear
Who's burst his cage, and, roaring here and there,

With hideous din, drives crowds before his blether,
Both ignorant and learnèd, hell-for-leather.
If some poor devil falls into his grip
He hugs him to his heart and then lets rip
And will not cease till death. So leeches suck
And, till they're gorged, will never come unstuck.

PART THREE

St. John of the Cross

Upon a Gloomy Night

Upon a gloomy night,
With all my cares to loving ardours flushed,
(O venture of delight!)
With nobody in sight
I went abroad when all my house was hushed.

In safety, in disguise,
In darkness up the secret stair I crept,
(O happy enterprise)
Concealed from other eyes
When all my house at length in silence slept.

Upon that lucky night
In secrecy, inscrutable to sight,
I went without discerning
And with no other light
Except for that which in my heart was burning.

It lit and led me through
More certain than the light of noonday clear
To where One waited near
Whose presence well I knew,
There where no other presence might appear.

Oh night that was my guide!
Oh darkness dearer than the morning's pride,
Oh night that joined the lover
To the beloved bride
Transfiguring them each into the other.

Within my flowering breast
Which only for himself entire I save
He sank into his rest
And all my gifts I gave
Lulled by the airs with which the cedars wave.

Over the ramparts fanned
While the fresh wind was fluttering his tresses,
With his serenest hand
My neck he wounded, and
Suspended every sense with its caresses.

Lost to myself I stayed
My face upon my lover having laid
From all endeavour ceasing:
And all my cares releasing
Threw them amongst the lilies there to fade.

*

Verses written after an ecstasy of high exaltation

I entered in. I know not where,
And I remained, though knowing naught,
Transcending knowledge with my thought.

Of when I entered I know naught,
But when I saw that I was there
(Though where it was I did not care)
Strange things I learned, with greatness fraught.
Yet what I heard I'll not declare.
But there I stayed, though knowing naught,
Transcending knowledge with my thought.

Of peace and piety interwound
This perfect science had been wrought,
Within the solitude profound
A straight and narrow path it taught,
Such secret wisdom there I found
That there I stammered, saying naught,
But topped all knowledge with my thought.

So borne aloft, so drunken-reeling,
So rapt was I, so swept away,
Within the scope of sense or feeling

My sense or feeling could not stay.
And in my soul I felt, revealing,
A sense that, though its sense was naught,
Transcended knowledge with my thought.

The man who truly there has come
Of his own self must shed the guise;
Of all he knew before the sum
Seems far beneath that wondrous prize:
And in this lore he grows so wise
That he remains, though knowing naught,
Transcending knowledge with his thought.

The farther that I climbed the height
The less I seemed to understand
The cloud so tenebrous and grand
That there illuminates the night.
For he who understands that sight
Remains for aye, though knowing naught,
Transcending knowledge with his thought.

This wisdom without understanding
Is of so absolute a force
No wise man of whatever standing
Can ever stand against its course,
Unless they tap its wondrous source,
To know so much, though knowing naught,
They pass all knowledge with their thought.

This summit all so steeply towers
And is of excellence so high
No human faculties or powers
Can ever to the top come nigh.
Whoever with its steep could vie,
Though knowing nothing, would transcend
All thought, forever, without end.

If you would ask, what is its essence—
This summit of all sense and knowing:
It comes from the Divinest Presence—

The sudden sense of Him outflowing,
In His great clemency bestowing
The gift that leaves men knowing naught,
Yet passing knowledge with their thought.

★

Coplas about the soul which suffers with impatience to see God

I live without inhabiting
Myself—in such a wise that I
Am dying that I do not die.

Within myself I do not dwell
Since without God I cannot live.
Reft of myself, and God as well,
What serves this life (I cannot tell)
Except a thousand deaths to give?
Since waiting here for life I lie
And die because I do not die.

This life I live in vital strength
Is loss of life unless I win You:
And thus to die I shall continue
Until in You I live at length.
Listen (my God!) my life is in You.
This life I do not want, for I
Am dying that I do not die.

Thus in your absence and your lack
How can I in myself abide
Nor suffer here a death more black
Than ever was by mortal died.
For pity of myself I've cried
Because in such a plight I lie
Dying because I do not die.

The fish that from the stream is lost
Derives some sort of consolation
That in his death he pays the cost
At least of death's annihilation.
To this dread life with which I'm crossed
What fell death can compare, since I,
The more I live, the more must die.

When thinking to relieve my pain
I in the sacraments behold You
It brings me greater grief again
That to myself I cannot fold You.
And that I cannot see you plain
Augments my sorrows, so that I
Am dying that I do not die.

If in the hope I should delight,
Oh Lord, of seeing You appear,
The thought that I might lose Your sight,
Doubles my sorrow and my fear.
Living as I do in such fright,
And yearning as I yearn, poor I
Must die because I do not die.

Oh rescue me from such a death
My God, and give me life, not fear;
Nor keep me bound and struggling here
Within the bonds of living breath.
Look how I long to see You near,
And how in such a plight I lie
Dying because I do not die!

I shall lament my death betimes,
And mourn my life, that it must be
Kept prisoner by sins and crimes
So long before I am set free:
Ah God, my God, when shall it be?
When I may say (and tell no lie)
I live because I've ceased to die?

★

Other verses with a
divine meaning by the same author

Not without hope did I ascend
Upon an amorous quest to fly
And up I soared so high, so high,
I seized my quarry in the end,

As on this falcon quest I flew
To chase a quarry so divine,
I had to soar so high and fine
That soon I lost myself from view.
With loss of strength my plight was sorry
From straining on so steep a course.
But love sustained me with such force
That in the end I seized my quarry.

The more I rose into the height
More dazzled, blind, and lost I spun.
The greatest conquest ever won
I won in blindness, like the night.
Because love urged me on my way
I gave that mad, blind, reckless leap
That soared me up so high and steep
That in the end I seized my prey.

The steeper upward that I flew
On so vertiginous a quest
The humbler and more lowly grew
My spirit, fainting in my breast.
I said 'None yet can find the way'
But as my spirit bowed more low,
Higher and higher did I go
Till in the end I seized my prey.

By such strange means did I sustain
A thousand starry flights in one,
Since hope of Heaven yet by none
Was ever truly hoped in vain.

Only by hope I won my way
Nor did my hope my aim belie,
Since I soared up so high, so high,
That in the end I seized my prey.

★

Romance III—Of the Creation

I wish to give You, My dear Son,
To cherish You, a lovely bride,
And one who for Your worth will merit
To live forever by Our side.

And she will eat bread at our table
The selfsame bread on which I've fed:
That she may know the worth and value
Of the Son whom I have bred,
And there enjoy with Me forever
The grace and glory that You shed.

'Thanks to You, Almighty Father,'
The Son made answer to the Sire,
'To the wife that You shall give Me
I shall give My lustrous fire,

'That by its brightness she may witness
How infinite My Father's worth
And how My being from Your being
In every way derived its birth.

'I'll hold her on My arm reclining
And with Your love will burn her so
That with an endless joy and wonder
Your loving kindness she may know.'

★

Romance IV

'Let it be done, then,' said the Father,
'For Your love's surpassing worth.'
And the moment he pronounced it
Was the creation of the Earth.

For the bride He built a palace
Out of His knowledge vast and grand,
Which in two separate compartments,
One high, one low, He wisely planned.

The lower storey was of endless
Differences composed: the higher
He beautified with wondrous jewels,
Refulgent with supernal fire.

That the bride might know her Bridegroom
In the true glory of His power,
In the top part He set the angels
In shining hierarchy to tower.

But, tenant of the lower mansion
Our human nature was assigned
Because its human composition
Falls short of the angelic kind.

And though the Being in two places
He divided in this way,
He composed of both one body
To house the Bride, who thus did say:

That the love of one sole Bridegroom
Made them into one sole Bride.
Those of the upper part possessed Him
In deathless joy beatified:

Those underneath, in hope and yearning,
Born of the faith He brings to birth,
By telling them that surely, sometime,
His love will magnify their worth;

And all in them that's base and lowly
He would exalt to such degree
That none who after that beheld it
Would scorn its first humility.

Exactly, in all things like they are,
He would cause Himself to be.
He would traffic in their dealings
And in their daily life agree.

And so the God would be the Man
And the Man be the God: and then
He would roam amongst them freely
And eat and drink with other men.

He will stay with us forever.
As a Comrade He will stay,
Till the present dispensation
Is consumed and fades away.

Then, to a deathless music sounding,
Bride to Bridegroom will be pressed,
Because He is the crown and headpiece
Of the Bride that He possessed.

To her beauty all the members
Of the just He will enlace
To form the body of the Bride
When taken into His embrace.

Tenderly in His arms He'll take her
With all the force that God can give
And draw her nearer to the Father
All in one unison to live.

There with the single, same rejoicing
With which God revels, she will thrill,
Revelling with the Son, the Father,
And that which issues from Their will,

Each one living in the other;
Samely loved, clothed, fed, and shod.
She, absorbed in Him forever,
She will live the Life of God.

★

Romance VIII—The same

Then He summoned an archangel,
Saint Gabriel: and when he came,
Sent him forth to find a maiden,
  Mary was her name.

Only through her consenting love
Could the mystery be preferred
That the Trinity in human
  Flesh might clothe the Word.

Though the three Persons worked the wonder
It only happened in the One.
So the Word was made incarnate
  In Mary's womb, a son.

So He who only had a Father
Now had a Mother undefiled,
Though not as ordinary maids
  Had she conceived the Child.

By Mary, and with her own flesh
He was clothed in His own frame:
Both Son of God and Son of Man
  Together had one name.

★

With a divine intention

Without support, yet well supported,
Though in pitch-darkness, with no ray,
Entirely I am burned away.

My spirit is so freed from every
Created thing, that through the skies,
Above herself, she's lifted, flies,
And as in a most fragrant reverie,
Only on God her weight applies.
The thing which most my faith esteems
For this one fact will be reported—
Because my soul above me streams
Without support, yet well supported.

What though I languish in the shades
As through my mortal life I go,
Not over-heavy is my woe,
Since if no glow my gloom invades,
With a celestial life I glow.
The love of such a life, I say,
The more benightedly it darkens,
Turns more to that to which it hearkens,
Though in pitch-darkness, with no ray.

Since I knew Love, I have been taught
He can perform most wondrous labours.
Though good and bad in me are neighbours
He turns their difference to naught
Then both into Himself, so sweetly,
And with a flame so fine and fragrant
Which now I feel in me completely
Reduce my being, till no vagrant
Vestige of my own self can stay.
And wholly I am burned away.

★

PART FOUR

Federico García Lorca

Romance of the Civil Guard of Spain

Their horses are as black as night
Upon whose hoofs black horseshoes clink;
Upon their cloaks, with dismal sheen,
Shine smears of wax and ink.
The reason why they cannot weep
Is that their skulls are full of lead.
With souls of patent leather
Along the roads they tread.
Hunchbacked and nocturnal,
You feel when they're at hand
Silences of india-rubber
And fears like grains of sand.
They travel where they like,
Concealing in their skulls of neuters
A blurred astronomy of pistols
And shadowy six-shooters.

O city of the gipsy people!
Flags at the corners of the streets.
With calabashes and the moon
And cherries candied into sweets.
O city of the gipsy people!
Who can forget you who has seen?
City of sorrow and of musk
With towers of cinnamon between.
When the night-time has arrived,
The night-time of the night,
Gipsy folk upon their anvils
Are forging suns and darts of light.
A wounded horse arrives and runs
To all the doors with plaintive whine.
Cocks of glass are crowing loud
At Jerez of the Frontier-Line.
Around the corner of surprise
The wind bursts naked on the sight,
In the night, the silver night-time,
In the night-time of the night.

The Virgin and Saint Joseph
Have left their castanets behind them
And come to ask the gipsies
If they will help to find them.
The Virgin like a Mayoress
Is sumptuously gowned
In silver chocolate paper
With almond necklets wound.
Saint Joseph moves his arms
In a silken cloak entwined
And with three Persian sultans
Pedro Domecq comes behind.
The crescent in the ecstasy
Of a white stork is dreaming
And over the flat roof-tops
Come flags and torches streaming.
Weeping before their mirrors
Hipless dancers mope and pine.
Water and shadow, shade and water
At Jerez of the Frontier-Line.

O city of the gipsies
With flags so fair to see,
Extinguish your green lamps, for here
Comes the Respectability!
O city of the gipsies
Who can forget you there?
Leave her distant from the sea
Without a comb to part her hair!

Two by two in double file
They reached the City of the Fair.
A sigh of everlasting flowers
Invades the cartridge-belts they wear.
A double nocturne of black cloth,
Their dark invasion naught deters.
Heaven to their approach appears
Merely a window-front of spurs.

The city multiplied its doors
Which, free from fear, had gaped asunder,

And through them forty Civil Guards
Enter to sack and plunder.
The clocks had stopped: the brandy
In bottles, with scared expedition,
Disguised itself with bleak November,
In order to avoid suspicion.
A flight of long-drawn screams
Ascended to the weathercock
While sabres cut the breeze with which
Their hoofs collide and shock.
The aged gipsy women fled
Along the twilight pavings,
Taking their drowsy horses
And pots filled with their savings.
Along the almost-upright streets
Sinister cloaks advance, all black
And leave a transitory vortex
Of whirling scissors in their track.

In the gateway of Bethlehem
The gipsies gather in a crowd.
Saint Joseph full of wounds,
Lays out a maiden in her shroud.
The sound of hard, sharp rifle-fire
Through all the darkness shocks and jars.
The Virgin cures the children
With the saliva of the stars.
But all the while the Civil Guard,
Advancing, sow the conflagration,
In which so tender, young, and naked,
Is roasted the imagination.
Rosa of the Camborios
Groans in a door beside the way
With her two amputated breasts
Beside her on a tray.
The other girls rush round
Chased by their flying hair
While roses of black powder
Burst round them in the air.

When all the roofs in furrows
Across the soil were strown
The morning swayed its shoulders
In a vast profile of stone.

O city of the gipsies!
The Civil Guard retires at last
Along the tunnel of the silence,
While the flames are mounting fast.

O city of the gipsies, who
That saw you could forget you soon?
Let them seek you in my forehead
The playground of the sands and moon.

★

Preciosa and the Wind

Beating upon the moon of parchment
Preciosa with her tambourine
Comes down by an amphibious path
Of laurel shade and crystal sheen.
The silence bare of any star,
Scared by the jangled sound she rings,
Falls where the deep sound of the ocean
Starry with fish, resounds and sings.
Amongst the peaks of the sierra
Slumber the coast-guard carbineers
Keeping a watch upon the towers
Where English folk have lived for years.
Beating on her moon of parchment,
Preciosa comes with rhythmic fall;
To see her come the rude wind rises,
The wind that does not sleep at all.
A huge Saint Christopher stark naked
Full of celestial tongues of air,
He looks upon the girl, and plays
On a sweet pipe that isn't there.

'Allow me, girl, to lift your skirt
And let me see you plain and clear.
Open to my ancient fingers
The blue rose of your beauty, dear!'

Preciosa flings away her tambour,
And runs, and runs, and does not tire
And the Big-Man-Wind pursues her
With a burning sword of fire.
The sea has puckered up its rumour,
All pale as death the olives grow.
The shrill flutes of the shadows sing.
So does the smooth gong of the snow.

Preciosa run! or the green wind
Will surely have you by the hair!
Run, Preciosa! run like mad!
Look out! He nearly got you there!
The satyr of the setting stars
With all his glittering tongues of air.

Preciosa, terrified to death,
Runs into the first house she sees,
Where high above the lofty pines,
The English Consul lives at ease.

Alarmed to hear her piercing screams
Come rushing down three carbineers
With their black cloaks hugged tightly round them
And caps pulled down about their ears.

A tumbler full of lukewarm milk
The Englishman provides in haste
And a goblet full of gin
Which Preciosa will not taste.

And while she tells her story weeping
And they are listening, without pause
Against the roof-top tiles above them
The wind in fury gnashed his jaws.

★

Reyerta

In the midst of the ravine,
Glinting Albacete blades,
Beautified with rival bloods
Flash like fishes in the shades.
A hard flat light of playing cards
Outlines, against the bitter green,
Shapes of infuriated horses
And profiles of equestrian mien.
Under the branches of an olive,
Weep two women bent with age,
While the bull of altercation
Clambers up the walls with rage.
Black angels come with handkerchiefs
And water from the snowline-boulders,
Angels with vast wings, like the blades
Of Albacete, on their shoulders.
Juan Antonio from Montilla
Down the slope goes rolling dead,
With his flesh stuck full of lilies,
A sliced pomegranate for his head;
And now the cross of fire ascends
Along the highways of the dead.

The Judge and Civil Guard their way
Along the olive orchard take,
Where slithered blood begins to moan
The dumb song of an injured snake.
'Gentleman of the Civil Guard!
The same old story as before—
Five of the Carthaginians slain
And of the Roman people four.'
The maddening afternoon of figtrees
And of hot rumours, ending soon,
Fell down between the wounded thighs
Of the wild horsemen in a swoon.
Black angels fly across the air
From which the setting sun departs,

Angels with long dark streaming hair
And oil of olives in their hearts.

★

Somnambulistic Ballad

Green, green, how deeply green![1]
Green the wind and green the bough,
The ship upon the ocean seen,
The horse upon the mountain's brow.
With the shadows round her waist
Upon her balcony she dreams.
Green her flesh and green her tresses,
In her eyes chill silver gleams.
Green, green, how deeply green,
While the gipsy moonbeam plays
Things at her are gazing keenly
But she cannot meet their gaze.

Green, green, how deeply green!
See the great stars of the frost
Come rustling with the fish of shadow
To find the way the dawn has lost.
The figtree chafes the passing wind
With the sandpaper of its leaves,
And hissing like a thievish cat,
With bristled fur, the mountain heaves.
But who will come? And by what path?
On her verandah lingers she,
Green her flesh and green her hair,
Dreaming of the bitter sea.

'Companion, I should like to trade
My pony for your house and grange,
To swap my saddle for your mirror,
My sheath-knife for your rug to change.'

[1] Literally 'Green, green, I want you green': but it has this secondary
meaning too.

'Companion, I have galloped bleeding
From Cabra's passes down the range.'
'If it could be arranged, my lad,
I'd clinch the bargain; but you see
Now I am no longer I,
Nor does my house belong to me.'
'Companion, I should like to die
Respectably at home in bed,
A bed of steel if possible,
With sheets of linen smoothly spread.
Can you not see this gash I carry
From rib to throat, from chin to chest?'
'Three hundred roses darkly red
Spatter the white front of your vest.
Your blood comes oozing out to spread,
Around your sash, its ghostly smell.
But now I am no longer I
Nor is my house my own to sell.'
'Let me go up tonight at least,
And climb the dim verandah's height.
Let me go up! O let me climb
To the verandah green with light!
O chill verandahs of the moon
Whence fall the waters of the night!'

And now the two companions climb
Up where the high verandah sheers,
Leaving a little track of blood
Leaving a little trail of tears.
Trembling along the roofs, a thousand
Sparkles of tin reflect the ray.
A thousand tambourines of glass
Wounded the dawning of the day.

Green, green, how deeply green!
Green the wind and green the bough.
The two companions clambered up
And a long wind began to sough
Which left upon the mouth a savour
Of gall and mint and basil-flowers.

'Companion! Tell me. Where is she?
Where is that bitter girl of ours?'
'How many times she waited for you!
How long she waited, hoped, and sighed,
Fresh her face, and black her tresses,
Upon this green verandah-side!'

Over the surface of the pond
The body of the gipsy sways.
Green her flesh, and green her tresses,
Her eyes a frosty silver glaze.
An icicle hung from the moon
Suspends her from the water there.
The night became as intimate
As if it were the village square.
The drunkards of the Civil Guard
Banging the door, began to swear.
Green, O green, how deeply green!
Green the wind and green the bough,
The ship upon the waters seen,
The horse upon the mountain's brow.

★

Ballad of the Black Sorrow

O Soledad of all my sorrows,
Like a stampeding horse that raves
And when it meets the sea at last
Is swallowed outright by the waves!
'Do not remind me of the sea
That with the same black sorrow grieves
Over the country of the olives
Under the rumour of the leaves.'

In the fresh water of the larks
Refresh your body, and release
Your weary heart, O Soledad
Montoya! to repose in peace.

69

Away down there the river sings
The skirt-flounce of the sky and leaves.
Crowning itself with pumpkin flowers
The new light rustles through the sheaves.
O sorrow of the gipsy people,
Clean sorrow lonely as a star,
O sorrow of the hidden fountain
And of the daybreak seen afar!

★

Saint Michael

From the verandahs they are seen
Along the rocky mountain tracks—
Mules, and the shadows of the mules,
With loads of sunflowers on their backs.

His eyes amongst the shadows
Are tarnished with enormous night
And up the spirals of the air
Passes the dawn with salty light.

A sky of mules as white as milk
Closes its glazed, mercurial eyes
Imposing on the twilight hush
A period to hearts and sighs.
The water makes itself so cold
That nobody to touch it dares,
Mad water, running naked stark
Along the rocky mountain stairs.
Saint Michael, laden with his laces,
In the church-alcove where he camps
Is showing off his lordly thighs
Surrounded by a ring of lamps.

Archangel of domestic meekness,
When the stroke of midnight rings
He feigns a sweet fictitious anger
Of nightingales and rustling wings.

He sings amongst the stained glass windows,
Ephebus of three thousand eves
Fragrant with water of Cologne
But far away from flowers and leaves.

Waves on the shore compose a poem;
Each in its window-bay rejoices:
The river borders of the moon
Lose in reeds to gain in voices.
Flashy 'monolas' from the slums
Come chewing sunflower seeds and pips
With their occult, enormous bums
Like brazen planets in eclipse.
Tall gentlemen come down the way
With ladies sorrowful and frail
Wan with the thoughts of yesterday
And memories of the nightingale.

And the Bishop of Manila,
So poor and saffron-blinded, then
Says a Mass which has two edges
One for the women, one for men.

Saint Michael stayed content and quiet
Up in his garret in the tower
In his skirts, cascading finery,
Where crystals, lace and trinkets shower,
Saint Michael, ruler of the lamps,
And of the Offices and Paters,
Poised in the Berber eminence
Of crowds and wondering spectators.

★

Saint Rafael

Along the riverside of reeds
Closed carriages assemble, where
The waves are polishing the bronze
Of Roman torsos brown and bare:

Carriages that the Guadalquivir
Portrays upon her ancient glass
Between the colour-plates of flowers
And thunders of the clouds that pass.
The lads are weaving as they sing
The disillusion of the world
Around the ancient carriages
By the encroaching darkness furled.
But Córdoba stirs not, nor trembles
Under the mystery they invoke,
Since, if the darkness were to shift
The architecture of the smoke,
With marble foot she reasserts
Her glory spotless and severe.
A flimsy petal-work of silver
Encrusts the breeze so grey and clear
Above the great triumphal arches
Displayed upon the atmosphere.
And while the bridge sighs out its ten
Reverberations of the sea,
Contrabanders of tobacco
Between the broken ramparts flee.

A single fish within the water,
Links the two Córdobas and joins
The gentle Córdoba of reeds
To that of architraves and groins.
Lads with expressionless blank faces
Along the bank strip to the skin,
Apprentices of Saint Tobias
And belted rivals of Merlin,
To tease the fish with taunting queries
Whether it would prefer more soon
Red splashes of the flowers of wine
Or acrobatics of the moon.
But the fish that gilds the water
And makes the marble dark and solemn,
Instructs them in the equilibrium

Of a solitary column.
The Archangel, arabianised,
With gloomy spangles all around,
In the mass-meeting of the waves
Sought out a cradle in their sound.

A single fish within the water,
Two Córdobas in beauty clear.
Córdoba broken into streams.
Córdoba heavenly and austere.

★

Saint Gabriel

A lad as graceful as a reed
With shoulders broad and body slight,
With a skin of moonlit apples,
Sad mouth, and large eyes brimmed with light,
Like a nerve of burning silver
Round the deserted streets and square;
His shining shoes of patent leather
Trample the dahlias of the air
With their two rhythms that resound
Celestial dirges as they pace.
On all the seacoast is not found
A palm to equal him in grace,
Nor emperor that wears a crown,
Nor any wandering star in space.
When to his jasper breast he stoops
His forehead in that pensive way,
The night seeks out the lowliest plain
Because she wants to kneel and pray.
For the Archangel Gabriel
Lonely guitars sing on the breeze,
The tamer of the turtle-doves
And enemy of the willow-trees.
—Saint Gabriel, the child is weeping
Within his mother's womb alone.
Do not forget the suit of clothes
The gipsies gave you as your own.

Annunciation of the Kings,
So richly mooned, so poorly dressed,
Opens the door into the street
To entertain her starry guest.
The archangel Saint Gabriel,
Between a lily and a smile,
Great-grandson of the high Giralda,
Had been approaching all this while.
In the embroidery of his jacket
The crickets palpitate and sing
And all the stars that lit the night,
Turning to bells, began to ring.
'Saint Gabriel, you see me here
Pierced with three nails of fierce delight.
Your glory from my burning face
Suns forth the jasmines opening white.'
'God is with you, Annunciation,
Brown beauty of the gipsy kind,
You'll have a son more beautiful
Than rushes waving in the wind.'
'Saint Gabriel, dearer than my eyes,
Dear Gabriel of my days and hours!
To seat you here I visualise
A bank of sweet carnation flowers.'
'God is with you, Annunciation,
So richly mooned, so poorly dressed,
Your son will have a little mole
And three red gashes on his chest.'
'Saint Gabriel, how your glory shines!
Dear Gabriel of my life and veins!
Down in the bottom of my breasts
I feel the warm white milk that drains.'
'God is with you, Annunciation,
Mother of dynasties without end!
Your eyes burn like the barren plains
Through which the lonely horsemen wend.'
The baby sings within the breast
Annunciation to surprise.
Three seedlets of the almond green
Are trembling in his tiny cries.

Saint Gabriel through the silent air
Went up a ladder to the sky;
And all the stars of night were turned
To everlasting flowers on high.

★

The Death of Antonio el Camborio

Voices along the Guadalquivir,
Were heard. Old voices, croaking death,
Surround and trap the manly voice
With the carnations in his breath.
He bit the boots that stove his ribs
With slashes of a tusky boar.
He bucked the soapy somersaults
Of dolphins, slithering in his gore.
He dyed in his opponents' blood
The crimson necktie that he wore,
But then there were four knives to one
So in the end he could no more.
When in the grey bull of the water
Stars strike their javelins; in the hours
When yearling calves are softly dreaming
Veronicas[1] of gillyflowers,
Voices of death re-echoed screaming
Along that river bank of ours.

Antonio, of Camborio's clan,
That have blue manes both thick and strong,
With olive skins, like moonlight green,
And red carnations in their song,
Beside the Guadalquivir's shore,
Who took your life, who could it be?
'The four Heredias, my cousins,
The children of Benamejí.
Things which they did not grudge to others
Were things for which they envied me—

[1] Veronica is a pass in bullfighting.

75

My shoes of bright Corinthian hue,
My medals made of ivory,
And this fine skin, in which the olive
And jasmine both so well agree.'
'Alas, Antonio el Camborio,
So worthy of an empress high,
Remember now to pray the Virgin
Because you are about to die.'
'Ah! Federico García Lorca,
Go quickly while there's time, and raise
The Civil Guard for I am broken
And wilting like a stalk of maize.'

He had three leakages of blood
And then, in profile, there he died,
Live currency of gold whose like
Can never be again supplied.
A withered angel came and placed
A pillow underneath his head,
While others with a weary flush
Lit up a candle for the dead.
And when the four Heredia cousins
Back to Benamejí had come,
Voices of death along the river
Ceased to be heard: and all was dumb.

★

He died of Love

'What is that thing that blazed there
Along the corridors in heaven?'
'Come in, my lad, and close the door;
Already it has struck eleven.'
'Within my eyes, against my will,
Four blazing torches seem to pass.'
'It must be that the people yonder
Have started polishing their brass.'

A garlic-slice of sickly silver,
It seems the waning moon has thrown
Heads of hair with yellow tresses
Over the towers of yellow stone.
The night along the balconies
Calls trembling at the window-glasses,
Bayed after by a thousand dogs
Who do not know her as she passes.
A scent of ambergris and wine
Floats from the corridors on high.

Breezes from the dewy reeds,
With many a lost archaic cry,
Reverberated in the broken
Archway of the midnight sky.
Oxen and roses were asleep,
But through the corridors, four lights,
With all the fury of Saint George,
Vociferated in the heights.
Sad women from the valley came
Bearing their manly strength of blood,
Assuaged in the cut flower, and bitter
In the thighs of youthful bud;
Old women of the riverside
Wept in the valley for the flames
Of the intransitable moment
Of waving hair and whispered names.
Façades of whitewash cut the dark
And squared it off, abrupt and white.
The seraphim and gipsy people
Played their accordions in the night.

'Mother, when I am dead, to all
The gentlefolk proclaim it forth.
Let azure telegrams be sent
Travelling from the South to North.'
Seven cries, and seven bloods,
And seven poppies (double blooms)
Smashed the unreflecting mirrors
That tarnished in the darkened rooms.

Full of amputated hands
And funeral wreaths, in vast despair,
The ocean-flood of perjured oaths
Was thundering—I don't know where.
Heaven slammed its doors against the rumour
With which the forests heave and cry,
While the four lights vociferated
Along the corridors on high.

★

Fable

Unicorns and cyclopses.

Horns of gold
and eyes of green.

Over the steep
in giant confusion
they illustrate the unglazed
mercury of the sea.

Unicorns and cyclopses.

An eyeball
and a power.

Who doubts the terrible
efficiency of those horns?

Nature!
Conceal your targets.

★

Song of the Horseman

Córdoba.
Remote and lonely.

Jet-black mare and full round moon,
With olives in my saddle bags,

Although I know the road so well
I shall not get to Córdoba.

Across the plain, across the wind,
Jet-black mare and full red moon,
Death is gazing down upon me,
Down from the towers of Córdoba.

Ay! The road so dark and long.
Ay! My mare so tired yet brave.
Death is waiting for me there
Before I get to Córdoba.

Córdoba.
Remote and lonely.

★

Sonnet—*Tall silver ghost, the wind of midnight sighing*

Tall silver ghost, the wind of midnight sighing
In pity opened up my ancient wound
With his grey hand: then went and left me lying
Where with my own sad longing I had swooned.

This wound will give me life: from it will come
Pure light and blood that issues without rest,
A rift wherein the nightingale, now dumb,
May find a grove, a sorrow, and a nest.

O what a gentle rumour stirs my brain!
Beside the simplest flower I'll lay my pain
Where floats, without a soul, your beauty's pride.

Then to a ruddy gold will change the vagrant
Stream, as my blood flows out into the fragrant
Dew-sprinkled thickets of the riverside.

★

Adam

The morning by a tree of blood was dewed
And near to it the newborn woman groans.
Her voice left glass within the wound, and strewed
The window with a diagram of bones.

Meanwhile the day had reached with steady light
The limits of the fable, which evades
The tumult of the bloodstream in its flight
Towards the dim cool apple in the shades.

Adam, within the fever of the clay,
Dreams a young child comes galloping his way,
Felt in his cheeks, with double pulse of blood.

But a dark other Adam dreaming yearned
For a stone neuter moon, where no seeds bud,
In which that child of glory will be burned.

★

PART FIVE

Other Spanish Poems

On Lisi's Golden Hair—Quevedo
(translated for Edith Sitwell)

When you shake loose your hair from all controlling,
Such thirst of beauty quickens my desire
Over its surge in red tornadoes rolling
My heart goes surfing on the waves of fire.
Leander, who for love the tempest dares,
It lets a sea of flames its life consume:
Icarus, from a sun whose rays are hairs,
Ignites its wings and glories in its doom.
Charring its hopes (whose deaths I mourn) it strives
Out of their ash to fan new phoenix-lives
That, dying of delight, new hopes embolden.
Miser, yet poor, the crime and fate it measures
Of Midas, starved and mocked with stacks of treasures,
Or Tantalus, with streams that shone as golden.

★

On a Chaplain's Nose—Quevedo

Limblike to his own snout, projecting there,
A man was hung. Sufficient it appeared
For all the scribes and pharisees to share,
Protruding like a swordfish from his beard.
It seemed an ill-set dial-hand, a pensile
Alembic, or an elephant, whose hose
Is turned the wrong way up, and less prehensile.
Ovid's was far less noseyfied a nose.

It seems the beak and ram of some huge galley,
Or pyramid of Egypt. The Twelve Tribes
Of noses it exceeds and circumscribes.
For sheer nasality it has no tally.
A nose so fiercely nasal in its bias
Would even spoil the face of Ananias.

★

You a Wing among the Wings of Birds—
José-Maria Alonso Gamo

I trust to the return of birds who bring
Back to me what is lost, with homeward wing
Tenderly beating in the azure height.

Long-sought, they'll come, back from oblivion's verges
Like flakes of snow upon the wind that urges
To their old home the pulses of their flight.

The wanderers their cloistered home will seek,
Each laughing pinnace of the deep-sea surges
Or winged rapture of the virgin peak.

Along the starry paths their flight will shine
As on the deep green sorrow of the pine
The butterflies, that are the light of spring.

The softest feather in its downy prime
Upon the dawn's south winds will trill and chime
If of yourself an echo it should bring:

Dry southern winds, that sow with burning hands
Seeds of your breast in mine—the desert clime
Has lent to them the ardour of its sands:

Red clouds of daybreak gave them veins of blood:
And seas have scoured their deepest green recesses
Of sirens, nymphs, and dolphins of the flood.

What rapid flight! What urgent pulsing motion
If in its plumes, as captives, it caresses
Dreams of the shores that fringe your winged ocean!

What fleet endearments! What a steep, high kiss
Bursts shuddering in that soft air—surviving
(A miracle!) unwounded by its bliss.

What flock of lost, stray birds is wildly striving,
Rose of the cardinal four winds, deriving
Their own red dress from petals that it frays.

Far off the winter days their foreheads raise
To where the aura grows like daybreak, hiving,
As in a comb, the taste of honeyed rays.

Light falling over light! Shot-silken glaze
That in your downy cheek delays arriving
There to become the wonder of the gaze.

Swift-glancing kiss! It offers me its gleam
Across the night of absence which my dream
Sustains against the fury of the wind.

Its azure, dim, transparency, confined
Thrall of the sky, refined you to a rare
And solitary pinion in the mind.

Flaked plume, no more, of ripening snows that run
Fusing into the soul the tuneful air
Of serenades the bird has just begun.

Wing of bright promise! Silken spectrum-blaze
Which an eternity shot through with rays
Showers with a thousand rose-petals of light.

Pinion of time itself! Upon whose flight
My prayer soars softly to the stars requiring
That one of them will bear it to your sight.

See them, the stars! With all their white aspiring
Wings flung wide open in a smile: they know
That I await you and they are desiring

To urge your flight and speed you as you go:
For all that there surround you—white snow-curds,
Aura, and yearning—turn to gales that blow,

And you a wing among the wings of birds.

★

On a White Foal dying on a Moonlit Night—
after Rafael Morales

Almost a zephyr: gale in adolescence:
Hot snow with wingèd tremors in its flight:
Warm moonbeam, stricken down in the quiescence
And coolness of a still, transparent night:
Your youthful head lies tenderly apart
As on the April verdure of a dream:
The frosty light peopled your rose-like heart
Too early with its snows. How freshly gleam
The mint and grass that for your pillow sprung,
But once to the carnation of your tongue
Gave fragrance, as it cropped them, crimson-petalled.
All has departed in the moon's chill beam.
Oh nubile, reckless head with mane astream!
Oh body of a wind the frost has settled!

★

To a Bull in Bronze—after Rafael Morales

Who could restrain the Spring from its mad rush
Or put the wind in gaol? Who could prolong
Into a century this moment's hush
In your horn'd brows, so menacing and strong?
The metal holds your fierceness captive surely
In breathless, closed rotundity of bronze.
Your motion is imprisoned there securely
By this new flesh your deathless anger dons.
You've halted to companion Time; your soul
Is captured in the bellow that you raise
With open jaws, along the sky to roll.
Out of these limits you shall never range,
Caught in that silent lasting bronze, your days
Withheld from all oblivion, death or change.

★

On the Skeleton of a Young Girl—
after Rafael Morales

Between these brows, Oh God, between these brows
Clamoured the living flesh! Here in this bleak
Hollow is where the red blood used to rouse
The fleeting roses of a youthful cheek.
Just here, the cunning breast gave forth its bud,
Adventurously shy, with grace and charm.
Here a delightful hand once pulsed with blood—
The offspring of that non-existent arm!
Here also did the swanlike neck sustain
The plumèd solitude that was her brain,
Fledged with her curls, like pinions wide and fleet.
And here in plump and lazy warmth extended
Her legs, like forking rivers, till they ended
To find the wing'd resilience of her feet.

★

From The Spectre of the Rose—Góngora

*Learn, flowers, from me, what parts we play
From dawn to dusk. Last noon the boast
And marvel of the fields, today
I am not even my own ghost.*

The fresh aurora was my cot,
The night my coffin and my shroud;
I perished with no light, save what
The moon could lend me from a cloud.
And thus, all flowers must die—of whom
Not one of us can cheat the doom.

Learn, flowers, from me, etc.

What most consoles me for my fleetness
Is the carnation fresh with dew,

Since that which gave me one day's sweetness
To her conceded scarcely two:
Ephemerids in briefness vie
My scarlet and her crimson dye.

Learn, flowers, from me, etc.

The jasmine, fairest of the flowers,
Is least in size as in longevity.
She forms a star, yet lives less hours
Than it has rays. Her soul is brevity.
Could ambergris a flower be grown
It would be she, and she alone!

Learn, flowers, from me, etc.

The gillyflower, though plain and coarse,
Enjoys on earth a longer stay,
And sees more suns complete their course
As many as there shine in May.
Yet better far a marvel die
Than live a gillyflower, say I!

Learn, flowers, from me, etc.

To no flower blooming in our sphere did
The daystar grant a longer pardon
Than to the Sunflower, golden-bearded
Methusalem of every garden,
Eyeing him through as many days
As he shoots petals forth like rays.

Yet learn from me, what parts we play
From dawn to dusk. Last noon the boast
And marvel of the fields, today
I am not even my own ghost.

★

A Prayer to St. Christopher—Aurelio Valls

When the hero falls from the dizzy trapeze
He bounds and rebounds from a net which is suddenly there.
He leaps for the height with a whirling of arms and legs
But he cannot escape the ubiquitous triumphing mesh
Whose invisible spider expands and commands in the end.
The hero of most high flights is reduced to a puppet
Who clumsily strains for another, more fevered ascent.
In the hubbub of busy places, the quotidian noises
Seem hooks and cables amongst which a man is employed
With the sole idea of not losing his composure.
When he's kept with his fingers clamped under gigantic
Blocks of ministerial or commercial concrete
He must smile at all costs. If you've achieved the veneer
Of a more visible and cynical contentment
Than your brother-in-Christ who is caught in the selfsame trap,
He will feel diminished and your own lustre will increase
In the envy of the other sufferers.
Protect me, Saint, from belonging to the moment!
The smiles depart; yes, off they go already,
Trailing themselves painfully home to suburban squares,
To antiseptic edifices surrounded by flags of all nations,
At whose feet the death-rattle of the ultimate smile
Constitutes an event appointed for 5 p.m.
So the accursed hour caves in and crumbles.
But all things are not whelmed in its collapse.
I only gaze into the silence.
There is something taking shape like sediment
Within my heart—repose; the distances
Are of an urgent elemental substance
Whose mighty surface harmonizes slowly.
Love of the far-off daybreak.
Voiceless love for the absent woman.
Now I discern an open stretch of country
Peaceful in September;
Wide level land still glowing
With warmth of recent harvests;

High sacred upland country
Whereon the evening falls.
A hand descends to stroke the earth.
A vast bull's head bows down in death before it;
It is the sun. It falls on its knees before the silence,
And slowly, slowly, tilting like a pitcher,
Pours out into the dust its generous, overflowing life.

*

To a Millstone on the Ground—
Dionisio Ridruejo

The straight race of the prisoned water turned
A circle, and became your voice and theme,
Round loaf of rock, whose floury dances churned
The waters, gay with duckweed, of the stream.

Sun of the grain-ears, whose rotating lips,
Lips of the plain, that lightly kissed the corn,
Now hush the bitter springtime to eclipse
Like a dead moon amongst the flowers that mourn.

Today you lie, a wayside seat, quite still
Old coin of memory, lost change that tumbles
Amidst the homeless wreckage of the mill . . .

Sad Cyclops, eye without a glance, blind stare:
Formed like our destiny that rolls and rumbles
Transfixed upon the axle of the air.

*

Lisbon—Tirso de Molina

'I'll paint a picture of it in the air.'
'I'd like to hear it—someone fetch a chair.'
'Why, Lisbon is the world's eighth wonder.

90

Out of the inmost heart of Spain,
Which lies about the hills of Cuenca,
The Tagus rolls a sumptuous train,
And, having traversed half that country,
Then enters the Atlantic main,
Along the sacred banks of Lisbon's
Proud city on the southern side.
But just before its course and name
Get lost forever in the tide,
It forms a port on the Sierras,
Where ships of all the navies ride
That can be numbered in this world.
Like mustered pines in black battalions
The masts of dhows, feluccas, schooners
Of Turks, of Norsemen or Italians,
Of carracks, caravels and sloops,
Of barques and galleys, junks and galleons
Are crowded in such countless troops
They form a vast and flowering city
Where Neptune reigns, for miles inland!
Towards that part where sets the Sun,
Guarding the port on either hand
Of where the Tagus makes an entry,
(One called Cascais and one Saint John)
Two mighty fortresses keep sentry
With many a grimly snouted gun
Earth's mightiest strongholds each well able
The navies of the world to stun.
Just half a league from town there stands
Belem, the convent of Jerome,
Who for his guardian had a lion
And for his talisman a stone,
Whom Catholic and Christian princes
Are keeping their eternal home.
Passing the vast and splendid fabric
Beyond Alcantara, you sally
A league, to reach Jaregas Convent
Which fills a wide and lovely valley,

That is encircled by three slopes—
Here, with his paintbrush, would Apelles
Have to renounce his proudest hopes:
For seen far off, it seems as if
Clusters of pearls hang from the skies
Within whose clear immensity
Ten Romes appear to multiply
In labyrinths of convents, churches
And towers, with highways streaming by,
With many a vast estate and mansion
Extending to the sea and sky,
And all in infinite expansion,
Through Empires, sowing deathless seeds
Wherever thoughts of man can fly,
In building, missions, arts, in deeds
Of valour, verse that cannot die,
And flawless rectitude of law:
But reaching nearest to the sky
Of all the glories that I saw
The summit of her Christian pity
And most of all to be adored
The peak of the Imperial city
Her Hospital—Misericorde.
The thing most worthy of amaze
That in this wondrous pile I found
Was that from its high top the gaze
For seven leagues can sweep its rays
On sixty villages all round.
And all of them the sea through bays
Could reach, and at their doors was found.'

★

PART SIX

From Baudelaire's
Les Fleurs du Mal

To the Reader

Folly and error, avarice and vice,
Employ our souls and waste our bodies' force.
As mangy beggars incubate their lice,
We nourish our innocuous remorse.

Our sins are stubborn, craven our repentance.
For our weak vows we ask excessive prices.
Trusting our tears will wash away the sentence,
We sneak off where the muddy road entices.

Cradled in evil, that Thrice-Great Magician,
The Devil, rocks our souls, that can't resist;
And the rich metal of our own volition
Is vapourised by that sage alchemist.

The Devil pulls the strings by which we're worked:
By all revolting objects lured, we slink
Hellwards; each day down one more step we're jerked
Feeling no horror, through the shades that stink.

Just as a lustful pauper bites and kisses
The scarred and shrivelled breast of an old whore,
We steal, along the roadside, furtive blisses,
Squeezing them, like stale oranges, for more.

Packed tight, like hives of maggots, thickly seething,
Within our brains a host of demons surges.
Deep down into our lungs at every breathing,
Death flows, an unseen river, moaning dirges.

If rape or arson, poison, or the knife
Has wove no pleasing patterns in the stuff
Of this drab canvas we accept as life—
It is because we are not bold enough!

Amongst the jackals, leopards, mongrels, apes,
Snakes, scorpions, vultures, that with hellish din,
Squeal, roar, writhe, gambol, crawl, with monstrous shapes,
In each man's foul menagerie of sin—

There's one more damned than all. He never gambols,
Nor crawls, nor roars, but, from the rest withdrawn,
Gladly of this whole earth would make a shambles
And swallow up existence with a yawn . . .

Boredom! He smokes his hookah, while he dreams
Of gibbets, weeping tears he cannot smother.
You know this dainty monster, too, it seems—
Hypocrite reader!—You!—My twin!—My brother!

*

The Albatross

Sometimes for sport the men of loafing crews
Snare the great albatrosses of the deep,
The indolent companions of their cruise
As through the bitter vastitudes they sweep.

Scarce have they fished aboard these airy kings
When helpless on such unaccustomed floors,
They piteously droop their huge white wings
And trail them at their sides like drifting oars.

How comical, how ugly, and how meek
Appears this soarer of celestial snows!
One, with his pipe, teases the golden beak,
One, limping, mocks the cripple as he goes.

The Poet, like this monarch of the clouds,
Despising archers, rides the storm elate.
But, stranded on the earth to jeering crowds,
The great wings of the giant baulk his gait.

*

Elevation

Above the valleys and the lakes: beyond
The woods, seas, clouds and mountain-ranges: far
Above the sun, the aethers silver-swanned
With nebulae, and the remotest star,

96

My spirit! with agility you move
Like a strong swimmer with the seas to fight,
Through the blue vastness furrowing your groove
With an ineffable and male delight.

Far from these foetid marshes, be made pure
In the pure air of the superior sky,
And drink, like some most exquisite liqueur,
The fire that fills the lucid realms on high.

Beyond where cares or boredom hold dominion,
Which charge our fogged existence with their spleen,
Happy is he who with a stalwart pinion
Can seek those fields so shining and serene:

Whose thoughts, like larks, rise on the freshening breeze,
Who fans the morning with his tameless wings,
Skims over life, and understands with ease
The speech of flowers and other voiceless things.

★

Ill Luck

So huge a burden to support
Your courage, Sisyphus, would ask;
Well though my heart attacks its task,
Yet Art is long and Time is short.

Far from the famed memorial arch
Towards a lonely grave I come.
My heart in its funereal march
Goes beating like a muffled drum.

—Yet many a gem lies hidden still
Of whom no pick-axe, spade, or drill
The lonely secrecy invades;

And many a flower, to heal regret,
Pours forth its fragrant secret yet
Amidst the solitary shades.

★

The Giantess

Of old when Nature, in her verve defiant,
Conceived each day some birth of monstrous mien,
I would have lived near some young female giant
Like a voluptuous cat beside a queen;

To see her body flowering with her soul
Freely develop in her mighty games,
And in the mists that through her gaze would roll
Guess that her heart was hatching sombre flames;

To roam her mighty contours as I please,
Ramp on the cliff of her tremendous knees,
And in the solstice, when the suns that kill

Make her stretch out across the land and rest,
To sleep beneath the shadow of her breast
Like a hushed village underneath a hill.

★

Her Hair

O fleece that down her nape rolls, plume on plume!
O curls! O scent of nonchalance and ease!
What ecstasy! To populate this room
With memories it harbours in its gloom,
I'd shake it like a banner on the breeze.

Hot Africa and languid Asia play
(An absent world, defunct, and far away)
Within that scented forest, dark and dim.
As other souls on waves of music swim,
Mine on its perfume sails, as on the spray.

I'll journey there, where man and sap-filled tree
Swoon in hot light for hours. Be you my sea,
Strong tresses! Be the breakers and the gales
That waft me. Your black river holds, for me,
A dream of masts and rowers, flames and sails.

98

A port, resounding there, my soul delivers
With long deep draughts of perfumes, scent, and clamour,
Where ships, that glide through gold and purple rivers,
Fling wide their vast arms to embrace the glamour
Of skies wherein the heat forever quivers.

I'll plunge my head in it, half drunk with pleasure—
In this black ocean that engulfs her form.
My soul, caressed with wavelets there may measure
Infinite rockings in embalmèd leisure,
Creative idleness that fears no storm!

Blue tresses, like a shadow-stretching tent,
You shed the blue of heavens round and far.
Along its downy fringes as I went
I reeled half-drunken to confuse the scent
Of oil of coconuts, with musk and tar.

My hand forever in your mane so dense,
Rubies and pearls and sapphires there will sow,
That you to my desire be never slow—
Oasis of my dreams, and gourd from whence
Deep draughted wines of memory will flow.

★

The Balcony

Mother of memories, queen of paramours,
Yourself are all my pleasures, all my duty;
You will recall caresses that were yours
And fireside evenings in their warmth and beauty.
Mother of memories, queen of paramours.

On eves illumined by the light of coal,
The balcony beneath a rose-veiled sky,
Your breast how soft! Your heart how good and whole!
We spoke eternal things that cannot die—
On eves illumined by the light of coal!

How splendid sets the sun of a warm evening!
How deep is space! the heart how full of power!
When, queen of the adored, towards you leaning,
I breathed the perfume of your blood in flower.
How splendid sets the sun of a warm evening!

The evening like an alcove seemed to thicken,
And as my eyes astrologised your own,
Drinking your breath, I felt sweet poisons quicken,
And in my hands your feet slept still as stone.
The evening like an alcove seemed to thicken.

I know how to resuscitate dead minutes.
I see my past, its face hid in your knees.
How can I seek your languorous charm save in its
Own source, your heart and body formed to please.
I know how to resuscitate dead minutes.

These vows, these perfumes, and these countless kisses,
Reborn from gulfs that we could never sound,
Will they, like suns, once bathed in those abysses,
Rejuvenated from the deep, rebound—
These vows, these perfumes, and these countless kisses?

★

The Possessed

The sun in crêpe has muffled up his fire.
Moon of my life! Half shade yourself like him.
Slumber or smoke. Be silent and be dim,
And in the gulf of boredom plunge entire;

I love you thus! However, if you like,
Like some bright star from its eclipse emerging,
To flaunt with Folly where the crowds are surging—
Flash, lovely dagger, from your sheath and strike!

Light up your eyes from chandeliers of glass!
Light up the lustful looks of louts that pass!
Morbid or petulant, I thrill before you.

Be what you will, black night or crimson dawn;
No fibre of my body tautly-drawn,
But cries: "Beloved demon, I adore you!"

★

The Living Torch

Those lit eyes go before me, in full view,
(Some cunning angel magnetised their light)—
Heavenly twins, yet my own brothers too,
Shaking their diamond blaze into my sight.

My steps from every trap or sin to save,
In the strait road of Beauty they conduct me.
They are my servants, and I am their slave,
Obedient in whatever they instruct me.

Delightful eyes, you burn with mystic rays
Like candles in broad day; red suns may blaze,
But cannot quench their still, fantastic light.

Those candles burn for death, but you for waking:
You sing the dawn that in my soul is breaking,
Stars which no sun could ever put to flight!

★

The Cat

I

A fine strong gentle cat is prowling
As in his bedroom, in my brain;
So soft his voice, so smooth its strain,
That you can scarcely hear him miowling.

But should he venture to complain
Or scold, the voice is rich and deep:
And thus he manages to keep
The charm of his untroubled reign.

This voice, which seems to pearl and filter
Through my soul's inmost shady nook,
Fills me with poems, like a book,
And fortifies me, like a philtre.

His voice can cure the direst pain
And it contains the rarest raptures.
The deepest meanings, which it captures,
It needs no language to explain.

There is no bow that can so sweep
That perfect instrument, my heart:
Or make more sumptuous music start
From its most vibrant chord and deep,

Than can the voice of this strange elf,
This cat, bewitching and seraphic,
Subtly harmonious in his traffic
With all things else, and with himself.

2

So sweet a perfume seems to swim
Out of his fur both brown and bright,
I nearly was embalmed one night
From (only once) caressing him.

Familiar Lar of where I stay,
He rules, presides, inspires and teaches
All things to which his empire reaches.
Perhaps he is a god, or fay.

When to a cherished cat my gaze
Is magnet-drawn and then returns
Back to itself, it there discerns,
With strange excitement and amaze,

Deep down in my own self, the rays
Of living opals, torch-like gleams
And pallid fire of eyes, it seems,
That fixedly return my gaze.

★

Sorrow of the Moon

More drowsy dreams the moon tonight. She rests
Like a proud beauty on heaped cushions pressing,
With light and absent-minded touch caressing,
Before she sleeps, the contour of her breasts.

On satin-shimmering, downy avalanches
She dies from swoon to swoon in languid change,
And lets her eyes on snowy visions range
That in the azure rise like flowering branches.

When sometimes to this earth her languor calm
Lets streak a stealthy tear, a pious poet,
The enemy of sleep, in his cupped palm,

Takes this pale tear, of liquid opal spun
With rainbow lights, deep in his heart to stow it
Far from the staring eyeballs of the Sun.

★

The Owls

Within the shelter of black yews
The owls in ranks are ranged apart
Like foreign gods, whose eyeballs dart
Red fire. They meditate and muse.

Without a stir they will remain
Till, in its melancholy hour,
Thrusting the level sun from power,
The shade establishes its reign.

Their attitude instructs the sage,
Content with what is near at hand,
To shun all motion, strife, and rage.

Men, crazed with shadows that they chase,
Bear, as a punishment, the brand
Of having wished to change their place.

★

The Cask of Hate

The Cask of the pale Danaïds is Hate.
Vainly Revenge, with red strong arms employed,
Precipitates her buckets, in a spate
Of blood and tears, to feed the empty void.

The Fiend bores secret holes to these abysms
By which a thousand years of sweat and strain
Escape, though she'd revive their organisms
In order just to bleed them once again.

Hate is a drunkard in a tavern staying,
Who feels his thirst born of its very cure,
Like Lerna's hydra, multiplied by slaying.

Gay drinkers of their conqueror are sure,
And Hate is doomed to a sad fate, unable
Ever to fall and snore beneath the table.

★

Spleen

I'm like the King of some damp, rainy clime,
Grown impotent and old before my time,
Who scorns the bows and scrapings of his teachers
And bores himself with hounds and all such creatures.
Naught can amuse him, falcon, steed, or chase:
No, not the mortal plight of his whole race
Dying before his balcony. The tune,
Sung to this tyrant by his pet buffoon,
Irks him. His couch seems far more like a grave.
Even the girls, for whom all kings seem brave,
Can think no toilet up, nor shameless rig,
To draw a smirk from this funereal prig.
The sage who makes him gold, could never find
The baser element that rots his mind.

Even those blood-baths the old Romans knew
And later thugs have imitated too,
Can't warm this skeleton to deeds of slaughter,
Whose only blood is Lethe's cold, green water.

★

The Red-haired Beggar Girl

White girl with flame-red hair,
Whose garments, here and there,
Give poverty to view,
    And beauty too.

To me, poor puny poet,
Your body, as you show it,
With freckles on your arms,
    Has yet its charms.

You wear with prouder mien
Than in Romance a queen
Her velvet buskins could—
    Your clogs of wood.

In place of tatters short
Let some rich robe of court
Swirl with its silken wheels
    After your heels:

In place of stockings holed
A dagger made of gold,
To light the lecher's eye,
    Flash on your thigh:

Let ribbons slip their bows
And for our sins disclose
A breast whose radiance vies
    Even with your eyes.

To show them further charms
Let them implore your arms,
And these, rebuking, humble
    Fingers that fumble

With proffered pearls aglow
And sonnets of Belleau,
Which, fettered by your beauty,
   .They yield in duty.

Riffraff of scullion-rhymers
Would dedicate their primers
Under the stairs to view
    Only your shoe.

Each page-boy lucky starred,
Each marquis, each Ronsard
Would hang about your bower
    To while an hour.

You'd count, among your blisses,
Than lilies far more kisses,
And boast, among your flames,
    Some royal names.

Yet now your beauty begs
For scraps on floors, and dregs
Else destined to the gutter,
    As bread and butter.

You eye, with longing tense,
Cheap gauds for thirty cents,
Which, pardon me, these days
    I cannot raise.

No scent, or pearl, or stone,
But nothing save your own
Thin nudity for dower,
    Pass on, my flower!

★

The Seven Old Men

To Victor Hugo

Ant-seething city, city full of dreams,
Where ghosts by daylight tug the passer's sleeve.
Mystery, like sap, through all its conduit-streams,
Quickens the dread Colossus that they weave.

One early morning, in the street's sad mud,
Whose houses, by the fog increased in height,
Seemed wharves along a riverside in flood:
When with a scene to match the actor's plight,

Foul yellow mist had filled the whole of space:
Steeling my nerves to play a hero's part,
I coaxed my weary soul with me to pace
The backstreets shaken by each lumbering cart.

A wretch appeared whose tattered, yellow clothing,
Matching the colour of the raining skies,
Could make it shower down alms—but for the loathing
Malevolence that glittered in his eyes.

The pupils of his eyes, with bile injected,
Seemed with their glance to make the frost more raw.
Stiff as a sword, his long red beard projected,
Like that of Judas, level with his jaw.

He was not bent, but broken, with the spine
Forming a sharp right-angle to the straight,
So that his stick, to finish the design,
Gave him the stature and the crazy gait

Of a three-footed Jew, or crippled hound.
He plunged his soles into the slush as though
To crush the dead; and to the world around
Seemed less of an indifferent than a foe.

His image followed him (back, stick, and beard
In nothing differed) spawned from the same hole,
A centenarian twin. Both spectres steered
With the same gait to the same unknown goal.

To what foul plot was I exposed? of what
Humiliating hazard made the jeer?
For seven times (I counted) was begot
This sinister, self multiplying fear!

Let him mark well who laughs at my despair
With no fraternal shudder in reply . . .
Those seven loathsome monsters had the air,
Though rotting through, of what can never die.

Disgusting Phoenix, his own sire and father!
Could I have watched an eighth instalment spawn
Ironic, fateful, grim—nor perished rather?
But from that hellish *cortège* I'd withdrawn.

Perplexed as drunkards when their sight is doubled,
I locked my room, sick, fevered, chilled with fright:
With all my spirit sorely hurt and troubled
By so ridiculous yet strange a sight.

Vainly my reason for the helm was striving:
The tempest of my efforts made a scorn.
My soul like a dismasted wreck went driving
Over a monstrous sea without a bourn.

★

The Little Old Women

To Victor Hugo

I

In sinuous folds of cities old and grim,
Where all things, even horror, turn to grace,
I follow, in obedience to my whim,
Strange, feeble, charming creatures round the place.

These crooked freaks were women in their pride,
Fair Eponine or Lais! Humped and bent,
Love them! Because they still have souls inside.
Under their draughty skirts in tatters rent,

They crawl: a vicious wind their carrion rides;
From the deep roar of traffic see them cower,
Pressing like precious relics to their sides
Some satchel stitched with mottoes or a flower.

They trot like marionettes along the level,
Or drag themselves like wounded deer, poor crones!
Or dance, against their will, as if the devil
Were swinging in the belfry of their bones.

Cracked though they are, their eyes are sharp as drills
And shine, like pools of water in the night,—
The eyes of little girls whom wonder thrills
To laugh at all that sparkles and is bright.

The coffins of old women very often
Are near as small as those of children are.
Wise Death, who makes a symbol of a coffin
Displays a taste both charming and bizarre.

And when I track some feeble phantom fleeing
Through Paris's immense ant-swarming Babel,
I always think that such a fragile being
Is moving softly to another cradle.

Unless, sometimes, in geometric mood,
To see the strange deformities they offer,
I muse how often he who saws the wood
Must change the shape and outline of the coffer.

Those eyes are wells a million teardrops feed,
Crucibles spangled by a cooling ore,
Invincible in charm to all that breed
Austere Misfortune suckled with her lore.

Vestal whom old Frascati could enamour:
Thalia's nun, whose name was only known
To her dead prompter: madcap full of glamour
Whom Tivoli once sheltered as its own—

They all elate me. But of these a few,
Of sorrow having made a honeyed leaven,
Say to Devotion, "Lend me wings anew,
O powerful Hippogriff, and fly to heaven."

One for her fatherland a martyr: one
By her own husband wronged beyond belief:
And one a pierced Madonna through her son—
They all could make a river with their grief.

III

Yes, I have followed them, time and again!
One, I recall, when sunset, like a heart,
Bled through the sky from wounds of ruddy stain,
Pensively sat upon a seat apart,

To listen to the music, rich in metal,
That's played by bands of soldiers in the parks
On golden, soul-reviving eves, to fettle,
From meek civilian hearts, heroic sparks.

This one was straight and stiff, in carriage regal,
She breathed the warrior-music through her teeth,
Opened her eye like that of an old eagle,
And bared a forehead moulded for a wreath.

IV

Thus, then, you journey, uncomplaining, stoic
Across the strife of modern cities flung,
Sad mothers, courtesans, or saints heroic,
Whose names of old were heard on every tongue,

110

You once were grace, and you were glory once.
None know you now. Derisory advances
Some drunkard makes you, mixed with worse affronts.
And on your heels a child-tormentor prances.

But I who watch you tenderly: and measure
With anxious eye, your weak unsteady gait
As would a father—get a secret pleasure
On your account, as on your steps I wait.

I see your passionate and virgin crazes;
Sombre or bright, I see your vanished prime;
My soul, resplendent with your virtue, blazes,
And revels in your vices and your crimes.

Poor wrecks! My family! Kindred in mind, you
Receive from me each day my last addresses.
Eighty-year Eves, will yet tomorrow find you
On whom the claw of God so fiercely presses?

★

The Skeleton Navvy

I

Quaint anatomic plates are sold
Along the quays in third-hand stalls
Where tomes cadaverous and old
Slumber like mummies in their palls.

In them the craftsman's skill combines
With expert knowledge in a way
That beautifies these chill designs
Although the subject's far from gay.

One notes that, consummating these
Mysterious horrors, God knows how,
Skeletons and anatomies
Peel off their skins to delve and plough.

Navvies, funereal and resigned,
From the tough ground with which you tussle
With all the effort that can find
Filleted spine or skinless muscle—

O grave-snatched convicts, say what strange
Harvest you hope from such a soil
And who the farmer is whose grange
You would replenish with this toil.

Mean you to show (O evil-starred
Exponents of too stark a doom)
The promised sleep may yet be barred,
Even from us, beyond the tomb;

That even extinction may turn traitor,
And Death itself, can be a lie;
And that perhaps, sooner or later,
Forever, when we come to die,

In some strange country, without wages,
On stubborn outcrops delving holes,
We'll push a shovel through the ages
Beneath our flayed and bleeding soles?

★

The Dance of Death

To Ernest Christophe

Proud, as a living person, of her height,
Her scarf and gloves and huge bouquet of roses,
She shows such nonchalance and ease as might
A thin coquette excessive in her poses.

Who, at a ball, has seen a form so slim?
Her sumptuous skirts extravagantly shower
To a dry foot that, exquisitely trim,
Her footwear pinches, dainty as a flower.

The frills that rub her collarbone, and feel,
Like a lascivious rill against a rock,
The charms she is so anxious to conceal,
Defend them, too, from ridicule and mock.

Her eyes are forms of emptiness and shade.
Her skull, with flowers so deftly decked about,
Upon her dainty vertebrae is swayed.
O what a charm when nullity tricks out!

"Caricature", some might opine, but wrongly,
Whose hearts, too drunk with flesh that runs to waste,
Ignore the grace of what upholds so strongly.
Tall skeleton, you match my dearest taste!

Come you to trouble with your strong grimace,
The feast of life? Or has some old desire
Rowelled your living carcase from its place
And sent you, credulous, to feed its fire?

With tunes of fiddles and the flames of candles,
Hope you to chase the nightmare far apart,
Or with a flood of orgies, feasts, and scandals
To quench the hell that's lighted in your heart?

Exhaustless well of follies and of faults,
Of the old woe the alembic and the urn,
Around your trellised ribs, in new assaults,
I see the insatiable serpent turn.

I fear your coquetry's not worth the strain,
The prize not worth the effort you prolong.
Could mortal hearts your railleries explain?
The joys of horror only charm the strong.

The pits of your dark eyes dread fancies breathe,
And vertigo. Among the dancers prudent,
Hope not your sixteen pairs of smiling teeth
Will ever find a contemplative student.

Yet who's not squeezed a skeleton with passion?
Nor ravened with his kisses on the meat
Of charnels. What of costume, scent, or fashion?
The man who feigns disgust, betrays conceit.

O noseless geisha, unresisted gouge!
Tell these fastidious feigners, from your husk—
"Proud fondling fools, in spite of talc and rouge,
You smell of death. Anatomies of musk,

Withered Antinouses, beaux of dunder,
Corpses in varnish, Lovelaces of bone,
The dance of death, with universal thunder,
Is whirling you to places yet unknown!

From Seine to Ganges frolicking about,
You see not, through a black hole in the ceiling,
Like a great blunderbus, with funnelled snout,
The Angel's trumpet, on the point of pealing.

In every clime, Death studies your devices
And vain contortions, laughable Humanity,
And oft, like you, perfumes herself with spices
Mixing her irony with your insanity!"

★

Meditation

Be good, my Sorrow: hush now: settle down.
You sighed for dusk, and now it comes: look there!
A denser atmosphere obscures the town,
To some restoring peace, to others care.

While the lewd multitude, like hungry beasts,
By pleasure scourged (no thug so fierce as he!)
Go forth to seek remorse among their feasts—
Come, take my hand; escape from them with me.

From balconies of sky, around us yet,
Lean the dead years in fashions that have ceased.
Out of the depth of waters smiles Regret.

The sun sinks moribund beneath an arch,
And like a long shroud rustling from the East,
Hark, Love, the gentle Night is on the march.

★

PART SEVEN

Portuguese Poems

Love Song—At St. Simeon's shrine I sat down to wait—Mindinho

At St. Simeon's shrine I sat down to wait,
The waves came nearer, the waves grew great,
  As I was awaiting my lover,
  As I was awaiting my lover!
There at St. Simeon's shrine by the altar,
Greater and nearer, the waves did not falter,
  As I was awaiting my lover,
  As I was awaiting my lover!
As the waves drew nearer and greater grew,
There was no steersman nor rower in view,
  As I was awaiting my lover,
  As I was awaiting my lover!
The waves of the high sea nearer flow
There is no steersman, I cannot row
  As I am awaiting my lover,
  As I am awaiting my lover!
There is no steersman nor rower, and I
In the high sea in my beauty must die,
  As I am awaiting my lover,
  As I am awaiting my lover!
There is no steersman, no rower am I
And in the high sea my beauty must die,
  As I am awaiting my lover,
  As I am awaiting my lover.

★

Love Song—Tell me, my daughter, my pretty young daughter—Pero Meogo

Tell me, my daughter, my pretty young daughter,
What kept you so long at the fountain for water?
(I've fallen in Love)

Tell me my daughter, my beautiful thing,
What caused you to linger beside the cold spring?
(I've fallen in Love)
I loitered, dear mother, so long by the fountain
For stags had been coming to drink from the mountain.
(I've fallen in Love)
I waited so long for the water to clear
Because it was churned into mud by the deer.
(I've fallen in Love)
You are lying, my girl, for your lover, I think:
Since I saw no stag coming down to the brink.
(I've fallen in Love)
You are lying, my daughter, for love it must be,
For I never saw stag which could trouble the Sea.

★

My lover goes wounded—Pero Meogo

My lover goes wounded
And by my love struck
As by the king's keeper
Goes wounded a buck.
Oh mother, he goes,
By my love struck deeper
Than a buck wounded
By the head-keeper.
To drown in the sea
Goes the buck that is shot:
So will my friend
If I think of him not.
—Be guarded, my daughter,
I've seen such, with art,
Feigning for pity
To soften the heart.
Be guarded, my daughter,
I've known such, with skill,
Feigning for pity
To weaken the will.

★

Dance Song—Airas Nunes

Come let us dance, my friends, all three,
Under the flowering hazel tree,
For whoever is fair, as fair as we,
  If she have a lover,
Only the flowering hazel tree
  Will ever discover.

Dance now, my sisters, dance all three
Under this branch of the hazel tree,
For whoever is fine, as fine as we,
  If she have a lover,
Only this branch of the hazel tree
  Will ever discover.

By God, my friend, when there's naught else chancing,
Under this hazel tree come dancing.
For whoever looks well, as we look now,
  If she have a lover,
Only the overshadowing bough
  Will ever discover.

★

A scene from a play by Gil Vicente

What Every-Man does, and what No-One does

SCENE: Two Devils, Dinato and Belzebub.

BEL To get an estimate for sending
To Lucifer, our God and King,
Sit here and write down everything
We notice in the period pending—
For now the world is near its ending,
And that we may deserve our due
In the share-out, we must review,
And make a decent list, compending
All things that happen in our view.

*(Enter Every-Man—a man dressed as a rich
merchant and looking around, as if for
something he has lost. Then, after him,
enter a man dressed as a pauper, whose name
is No-One.)*

NO-ONE	What are you so intent to find?
EVERY-MAN	I go to seek a thousand things Whose getting never eased my mind— Still striving in persistence never brings.
NO-ONE	What is your name, sir, and your role?
EVERY-MAN	My name is Every-Man, My whole Existence is in seeking wealth. This task employs my time and health And is the function of my soul.
NO-ONE	My name is No-One. My one goal Is conscience.
BEL	Put that down in style And with a flourish. It's so funny!
DIN	Comrade, how shall I word the file?
BEL	'No-One follows his conscience, while Every-Man hunts around for money.'
NO-ONE	What now, sir, would you seek to see?
EVERY-MAN	My name renowned through all the land.
NO-ONE	I seek for virtue—as for me. And, look! I have it here to hand, As if it were by God's decree.
BEL	Another item. Note the same. These very words at once insert you!— That 'Every-Man goes chasing Fame, But No-One chases after Virtue.'
NO-ONE	No other blessing would you claim?
EVERY-MAN	Why, yes—that one and all should praise My slightest action, deed, or venture!
NO-ONE	And I—that one and all should censure The slightest error in my ways.
BEL	Write more!
DIN	But how would you have penned it?

BEL	That 'even to the extremest measure
	Every-Man in his praise takes pleasure,
	No-One in being reprehended!'
EVERY-MAN	I seek long life, and all who give it.
NO-ONE	I do not know, although I live it,
	What life is. Death is all I know.
BEL	Record that in a different breath.
DIN	How?
BEL	Why, far more waggishly and gaily!
	That 'Life by Every-Man is daily
	Pursued, while No-One thinks of Death.'
EVERY-MAN	I long for Paradise, with no
	Disturbance to my peace and joy.
NO-ONE	I long in penance to employ
	My soul—to pay the debt I owe.
BEL	Put that one down, and be precise.
DIN	The words, then?
BEL	This is how it goes:
	'While Every-Man wants paradise,
	No-One would pay the debt he owes.'
EVERY-MAN	I love to do a bit of cheating.
	Lying was born with me, I guess.
NO-ONE	The truth is what I love repeating—
	And never from its path digress.
BEL	Comrade, note that one down entire
	Quick, get it down, and don't be lazy!
DIN	What?
BEL	Write down that 'Every-Man's a liar,
	But No-One for the truth is crazy!'
EVERY-MAN	I love to fawn, and cringe, and flatter.
NO-ONE	For me such things are no great matter.
	I've no illusions on that score.
BEL	Write it!
DIN	But how to phrase the patter?
BEL	Quick! Mark it clearly to our score—
	And goggle at the ink no more!—
	That 'Every-Man delights to flatter,
	But No-One finds it all a bore.'

★

Rowing go the rowers—*Gil Vicente*

Rowing go the rowers
In a ship of great delight.
The captain at the helm
The Son of God is Light.
Angels at the oars
Rowed with all their might.
The flag of hope was flying
Lovely to the sight.
The mast was of endurance
Like crystal shining bright.
The sails were stitched with faith
And filled the world with light.
The seashore was serene
With not a wind in flight.

★

Canção IX—*Camões*

There is a mountain, sterile, stark and dry,
Useless, abandoned, hideous, bare and bald,
From whose cursed precincts nature shrinks appalled,
Where no beast ever sleeps, where no birds fly,
No river runs, nor bubbling sources spring,
Nor one green bough with pleasant sighs to sing.
In common speech the name they call it by
Is Felix[1] (unfelicitously given!)
By Nature it was placed
Just where a strait has riven
The Arabian from the Abyssinian waste,
Where Berenice used to stand of yore,
In that part of the shore
Where the sun, having burnt it, hides once more;

[1] Arabia Felix

Thence can be seen the Cape which ends the coast
Of Africa, which runs up from the south,
Called 'Aromatic' by as vain a boast
But something far less flowery in the mouth
Of the wild native in his savage tongue.
(Though fragrant once, perhaps, when time was young.)
There by the sea, whose high tide-swollen spate
Strives twice a day to burst that narrow strait,
To languish for a spell
It was my cursed fate,
There in that fierce inhospitable hell,
Where Life would fain desert itself to see
Its splintered bits, ah me!
Scattered about the world by land and sea.

Here was I stranded, passing dreary days,
Laborious evil, dolorous days and lonely,
Days full of toil, grief, rage, and long delays—
Not having for my adversaries only
Life, and the burning sun, and the chill tides,
With fierce, hot, roaring hurricanes besides,
But my own thoughts which only seemed my own
To play foul tricks on nature and deceive.
My memory too had grown
A thing to make me grieve,
Reviving some brief glories I had known
When in the world I sojourned, so to double,
By contrast, all my suffering and trouble,
By keeping me aware
That in the world were long hours free from care.

There did I live wasting both life and time
With these vain thoughts, which to a height immense
Reared me so steeply on their wings to climb
That so much steeper was my fall from thence,
Dashed downward from those castles in the air
To reach whose height I ever more despair.
Imagination here was turned to grief
In unexpected sobs to find relief
And sighs which rent the air.
My captive spirit there,

Wounded all over to the tender quick,
Crowded all round with sorrows dense and thick,
Unshielded lay beneath the hailing shot
Of my accursed lot,
Inexorable, fierce, and hell-begot.

There was not anywhere the least relief,
Nor any hope whereon to lay my head
And snatch a little rest, however brief.
All things for harm and suffering seemed bred
Save that I could not die: for to have died
Would baulk my angry fate, and was denied.
My groans made calm the stormy waves that rolled,
Importuned by my voice, the winds grew cold
Worn out with my lament.
Only the heavens cruel,
The stars, and fate, so fierce in its intent,
Found their amusement in the oft-renewal
Of my sad torments, showing off their spite
My wretched self to smite,
Poor earthly thing, and such a tiny mite!

O that amongst these labours I might only
Know that for certain I shall once behold,
But for one hour, two eyes I knew of old:
That my lament, so desolate and lonely,
Might reach the ears of that angelic sprite
Within whose view I lived in such delight:
And that she, turning backward in her mind,
Might, thinking of the times we've left behind,
Recall each sweet mistake,
Quarrel, or torment kind
I sought and suffered only for her sake:
And thus, remembering such things, were she
To feel a pang for me
And her own stony-heartedness to see:

Only to know this thing would mean, for me,
Peace through the rest of life that yet remains.
With that I could console my dreary pains.
Ah, Lady, Lady! Wealthy you must be
Since even to imagine you sustains,

Far from all pleasures, what remains of me
When in my thoughts your effigy I see
All pain and weariness turn tail and flee.
Alone your memory arms
My soul with fearless might
Against ferocious death and mortal harms.
New hopes come rushing to me from your charms,
New hopes, with which my brow serenely bright
Confronts the woes I fight
Turning them into memories of delight.

Here with these memories I remain, and sue
Of every amorous zephyr of the air
From your part of the world, some news of you.
I ask the birds which seem to fly from there
If they have seen you, when, and what you do,
What day and hour it was, with whom, and where.
Thus my tired life from day to day improves:
I win new spirits; something in me moves
Which conquers toil and fate
To feel that once again
I may return to see you at some date,
To love, and serve, and with you to remain.
Say when the time will come that ends my pain!
But my desire, that nothing can abate,
Pitiless as before,
Has opened up my suffering wounds once more.
Thus live I. If they ask you, Song, why I
Have not yet chance to die,
Tell them that I am dying: That is why.

★

The Sailor-Girl—Camões

Mother, my sighs unfurl
Forth on the seas to sally
With one in yonder galley
To be a sailor-girl.

O Mother mine, if only
I were where I would go!
I hate this Love so lonely,
This Love that loves him so,
This Cupid who's a churl,
This Babe who is my gaoler,
This longing for a sailor—
To be a sailor-girl!

He who all knots unravels
One he cannot unbind—
That though the spirit travels
The body stays behind.
With him for whom I'm dying
I'll go (or die—you'll see!)
All for a sailor trying
A sailor-girl to be.

What a despotic thing
The Tyrant Babe decreed
That One who is a King
For Love should have to bleed!
In such a wise, ah me!
Daily do I grow paler
For one who is a sailor
A sailor-girl to be.

Say, waves, if yet before
You ever saw so slender
A maiden, or so tender,
Go smiling from the shore!
From Babes that act the Demon
What mischiefs are not due?
To travel with my seaman
I'll be a sailor too!

★

From the Lusiads, Book VIII—Camões

Enduring now of Neptune, now of Mars,
The most inhuman perils and the scars,
Like Canace, self-sentenced and undone,
A pen in one hand, and a sword in one:
Now for my penury abhorred, evaded,
And now in foreign doss-houses degraded:
No sooner with a hope acquired, than straight
The deeper dashed from where I stood elate:
Now, with my life escaping on my back,
That hung upon a thread so thin and slack,
To save it was a miracle, no less
Than were our King for heathen to confess.
And yet, O Nymphs, these miseries, though great,
Suffice not to appease my angry fate,
Since all I've sung of others' woes and curses
Must be the prize and guerdon of my verses,
Replacing all the joys for which I yearn—
Honours, repose, and laurels: which to spurn,
New travails I have never proved before
Must be invented, and a thousand more.

★

On a shipmate,
Pero Moniz, dying at sea—Camões

My years on earth were short, but long for me,
And full of bitter hardship at the best:
My light of day sinks early in the sea:
Five lustres from my birth I took my rest.
Through distant lands and seas I was a ranger
Seeking some cure or remedy for life,
Which he whom Fortune loves not as a wife,
Will seek in vain through strife, and toil, and danger.

Portugal reared me in my green, my darling
Alanguer, but the dank, corrupted air
That festers in the marshes around there
Has made me food for fish here in the snarling,
Fierce seas that dark the Abyssinian shore,
Far from the happy homeland I adore.

★

Seven long years was Jacob herding sheep—Camões

Seven long years was Jacob herding sheep
For Laban, lovely Rachel's grim old father.
It was not for that mean old man, but rather
For her, he worked—the prize he longed to reap.
Days passed in expectation of one day.
That day of days became his sole idea.
But the old father swindled him with Leah
And gave him the wrong girl, with whom he lay.
The disillusioned shepherd, thus denied,
As if he'd never merited his bride,
Began another seven years' indenture.
Seven years more he laboured, staunch and strong,
Saying 'A longer contract I would venture—
But life's too short to serve a love so long.'

★

Dear gentle soul, who went so soon away—Camões

Dear gentle soul, who went so soon away
Departing from this life in discontent,
Repose in that far sky to which you went
While on this earth I linger in dismay.
In the ethereal seat where you must be,
If you consent to memories of our sphere,
Recall the love which, burning pure and clear,

So often in my eyes you used to see!
If then, in the incurable, long anguish
Of having lost you, as I pine and languish,
You see some merit—do this favour for me:
And to the God who cut your life short, pray
That he as early to your sight restore me
As from my own he swept you far away.

★

My being turns to smoke in the mad strife—Bocage

My being turns to smoke in the mad strife
Of passions which have whirled me in their wake.
How miserably blind was I to take
This human span for almost-endless life.
What countless suns the boastful fancy forges
To gild this false existence as it flows,
But now my slave-like nature undergoes
The blasting havoc of a life of orgies.

Pleasures, my tyrant cronies, in confusion,
Hurling you to the gulf of disillusion,
My thirsty soul no longer can be pent.
Before my light fails, grant, my God! that I,
(One moment saving what in years I spent),
Who knew not how to live, learn how to die!

★

Hymn of the Morning—Antero de Quental

You rise, O chaste and happy light of day,
And grow, vibrating purely in the height,
To fill triumphant hearts, who yet can pray
Or hope, with rays immaculately bright!

But in my heart, the home of desolation,
You pour enormous grief: since it prefers
The pitchblack Night, stark twin of desperation,
Dense, solitary, still, where no sound stirs.

The dumb void, where no star is seen to peep,
Where no bird sings, nor whispering breezes blow,
And thought itself falls heavily asleep—
To this clear morning light, this blessed glow!

Because the Night's the image of Non-Essence,
The image of unaltering repose,
Of undisturbed oblivion and quiescence,
For which the world yearns, weary with its woes.

For fixed and drowned in it, the darkness stores
The universal nothingness of thought,
And scorns this tortured world, which it ignores
As one already dead, and come to naught.

Intrepidly interrogating Doom,
Which, like a traitorous felon, it arraigns,
It turns once more towards the vacuous gloom,
Where, Godlike, grand, and peaceful, it remains—

Because the Night in truth's own image fashions
Itself, beyond our transitory range,
Hallucinating forms and fleeting passions,
Where only fraud and sorrow never change.

But you, O glorious light, so clear and fresh,
What do you symbolise, save the deceit
That in its myriad and mysterious mesh
Involves the world, as in a winding-sheet.

What do you stand for? Universal treason
And promises renewed to our confusion;
Still to be perjured in and out of season!
Mother of Life you are—and of Illusion!

Others stretch out their hands to you and pray,
With faith and hope, for what they never gain.
Others their wealth and confidence will lay
On promises, and days that dawn in vain.

I? No! On seeing you, I ask 'What sorrow
And what new torture yet unproven, say,
Will now be taught me by the breaking morrow?'
I ask, 'Why has it dawned another day?'

Of old you were not there, most lovely Light.
You had no being. The Universe, unwist,
Lay sunk inertly in the boundless night
Of possibility, a doubtful mist.

What do you bring with every dawn, save only
This feeling and this consciousness of ours
Of cureless, endless impotence, and lonely,
Insatiable hunger that devours?

Of what are made the loveliest of our morrows?
Of battles, lamentations, groans, and terrors!
Of what are made our days? Of countless sorrows,
Miseries, chagrins, agonies and errors!

The sun, a ruthless sower, without stop,
Tirelessly runs through space, and here and there
Out of his lap showers forth his fatal crop,
The innumerable harvest of despair.

See how that cursèd cornland swells and heaves
In the hot light, and how it shakes with fear
Before the winds of life! Hark how it grieves
In endless sighs, monotonous and drear!

Now, spread in rich voluptuous waves at length,
It grows with fierce fecundity, and breeds
With the same subtle and tenacious strength
That is invincible in noxious weeds.

From ancient filth its vigour is absorbèd.
It feeds on putrefaction in the mire.
A fragrance that is moribund and morbid
Seems from its poisoned sap-veins to perspire.

Composed of charms both hazy and magnetic,
Within this langorous aroma furled
Of carnal ardour and of charm poetic,
Was born the poison that infects the world.

Now like a trumpet-peal through hills and valleys,
The placid morning wakes, and drives to war
The miseries of earth. Their hosts she rallies
Horribly clamouring from shore to shore.

Grim, sightless, furious, famine-stricken, see!
They rush to arms, exchanging blow for blow
In brutal, endless strife, where all must be
Vanquished forever. But extinguished? No!

Though, at this hour, they raise new arms and shields,
In the bright morning, swelled with brutish force,
And seek the direst proofs that battle yields,
Gay, cruel, reckless, and without remorse—

Nightfall will see them trampled in the mud
And bleeding, as they vainly try to spew
At Heaven, through a gargled froth of blood,
The last foul imprecation that they knew.

How many, too, the night will overtake,
Lone and forgot, though still upon their feet,
And weeping, as they lean upon a stake,
Dumb tears of those who recognise defeat?

And why and wherefore do you call them, Light,
(Inexorable Light, serene and cruel!)
To this uncertain life and ruthless fight,
With your false visions firing them like fuel?—

Like toys within the playful hand of Doom
With which to while a fleeting day of mirth,
Or will-o-wisps that flicker, fade, and fume
Between the agonies of death and birth . . .

They seem, within the tedious firmament,
Blasted by evil stars with cheating light,
Like bands of piteous spectres that lament
Or shadows following a dream in flight.

Ah, no! Most glorious and triumphant whiteness,
Take off from me the glamour and the rays,
Of your great mantle of deluding brightness!
For to the sad and vacillating gaze

Of my tired eyes—all tarnished, dim and sick,
And bitter to my heart, appears the Day—
Like a forgotten torch whose dying wick
Lights up a monstrous charnel with its ray.

In vain with glory all around you ring me.
In vain you pierce me with a loving thrill.
You cause me fear. Horror is what you bring me!
I cannot love you, and I never will.

Symbolic of the Universal Guile,
The false appearances of fleeting shades,
Which Everlasting Evil, with a smile,
Disguises ere the swift perspective fades.

Symbol of Fraud! Out of the endless night
You made the Cosmos rise, already versed
In grief and evil, treachery and spite.
Symbol of all Existence! Be accurst![1]

*

[1] Translated in '43 while coast-watching in World War II on the
opposite coast by the "Gates of Hell" in full view of the "Monte
esteril". During this time the lighthouse keeper on Guardafui went mad
and had to be taken away.

The Most Holy Virgin—Antero de Quental

In a dream made of all that is uncertain,
Through long, unbroken hours of nightly pain,
I saw her pitying gaze, as through a curtain,
Where (more than pity) sorrow, too, was plain.

'Twas not the vulgar blaze of beauty's face,
Nor banal ardour that in youth we feel.
It was another light, another grace . . .
I know not even if it can be real . . .

A mystic suffering, which chanced to render
All pardon in its gaze, with all that's tender,
And peaceful as the hour when we expire.

O vision, sad and pitiful! Still keeping
This silence, stay with me. Remain, thus weeping;
And let me dream my life away entire.

★

The thing that hurts and wrings—
Fernando Pessoa

The thing that hurts and wrings
Was never in my heart.
It's one of those fair things
In life that have no part.

Shapes without shape—each shape
Seems silently to flit
Ere known by grief, and fade
Ere love can dream of it.

They are as if our grief
Were a dark tree from whom
They flutter leaf by leaf
Into the mist and gloom.

★

Death comes before its time—Fernando Pessoa

Death comes before its time,
Life is so brief a stay.
Each moment is the mime
Of what is lost for aye.

Life scarcely had begun,
Nor the idea diminished,
When he whose task was done
Knew not what he had finished.

This, doubting Death presumes
To cancel and to cut
Out of the book of dooms,
Which God forgot to shut.

★

The poet fancying each belief—Fernando Pessoa

The poet fancying each belief
So wholly through and through
Ends by imagining the grief
He really feels is true.

And those who read what he has spelt
In the read grief feel good—
Not in the two griefs he has felt,
But one they never could.

Thus to beguile and entertain
The reason, does he start,
Upon its rails, the clockwork train
That's also called the heart.

★

137

From the Maritime Ode—Alvaro de Campos

The whole quay is a memory in stone.
And when the ship leaves it, and suddenly
One sees the space widen
Between the quay and the ship,
I feel, I know not why, a recent anguish,
A haze of mournful feeling,
That shines in the sun of my grief
Like the first pane on which the morning shimmers.
It clothes me in the memory of another being
Whose person was mysteriously mine.

Who knows? Who knows if I have never
Embarked before, myself, from such a quay?
As a ship in the oblique rays of the morning sun, who knows
If I have not sailed from a different kind of port?
Who knows if I have not left (before the time
Of this exterior world as I behold it
Striping itself with colours for my sake)
A great Quay filled with the fewness of the people
Of as vast, as distended and apoplectic a city
As can exist outside of Space and Time.

Yes . . . from a quay in some way material,
Visible as a quay, real, and truly a quay,
The absolute Quay, from whose model, unconsciously were copied,
And insensibly evoked,
All the quays of our ports,
Our quays of actual stone in actual water,
Which, once constructed, announce themselves
As Real-Things, Spirit-Things, or Entities of the Stone-Soul,
Made ours at certain moments by root-sensations,
When in the outer world, as if a door were opened,
But altering nothing,
The All in its diversity is shown.

Ah, the great quay from which we sailed as Nation Ships!
The great Anterior Quay, eternal and divine!
From what port? In what waters? (Or else, how could I think it?)
A great Quay, like the others, but uniquely THE Quay,
Filled, like the rest, with rustling silences before the dawn,
And unwinding at daybreak in a roar of cranes and winches,
With trains arriving full of merchandise
Under the occasional, light cloud
Of smoke from nearby factories,
Which shadows its floor
Black with sequinned atoms that twinkle
As if it were the shade of a dark cloud
Passing over the face of black water.

★

Fear—Joaquim Paço d'Arcos

Fear is not dread of pirates on the river
Nor of the sea's typhoons.
It's not the dread of firing in the night
On the river thronged with treachery and junks.
It's not the dread of hanged men seen
In the white moonlight,
In the forest of mangoes of the Black Sand.
Fear's not the dread of hunger, war, or plague,
Nor of the lepers' scabs on Saint John's Island.
It is not the suspicion
That death is stalking us
Continually
And in the end will carry us away.

Fear is not the contagion of sorrow
When evening falls
And the sunset stains with blood
The muddy seashore,
The lands, and the sky,
Until these isles are swallowed up in shade
And the peaks in darkness

And nothing is left save the shadows
And cries traverse the night,
Coming from I know not whence,
Going I know not whither.

Fear is not dread of traps
Or daggers
Or of red kisses that betray
And slowly suck our lives . . .

Fear is the dread that you might go
And leave me here alone.

★

Re-encounter—Joaquim Paço d'Arcos

The jetty with its old wormeaten planks,
The cheerless sand-dunes and the ancient fort,
The desert that advances on the sea
Peppering the poor city with its yellow dust
And burying it in sand.

The vegetable gardens of Giraul,
A timid streak of green in sandy wastes,
The withered flowerbeds, burnt and dried,
By the fierce sun of Africa,
Destroy, when re-encountered thus, the image
Of the lush park which memory retained.
The little garden in the city,
Without its bandstand now,
But with its filing spectres,
Its long, interminable files of spectres . . .
Miss Blond out walking with her childish charges.
"Tiger", the dog, so mute and mild and sleepy.
The negroes with submissive, startled looks,
Walking with fettered feet
Through a street of mud-built huts and yielding earth.

Miss Blond no longer takes the children walking,
Tall, noble "Tiger" died of ripe old age,
The natives long ago destroyed their fetters,
Only the spectres have remained
Where they were left. They, only, populate
The memory and inhabit the town,
With their faint, beloved voices,
With their lost voices
In the deserted House, which now the desert
Covers with dust, and in this life, which time
Is covering with its dust,
In death, in memory, in death . . .

★

Irrigation—Francisco Bugalho

Slow, far, and melancholic,
With old songs still renewed,
The water-wheel goes round.
The breezes blow bucolic
(Lyrical solitude!)
And make my doors resound.

The thirsty air awaits
Yearningly all the day
Till afternoon returns,
And now the strain abates.
The kiss of the sun's ray
Warms, but no longer burns.

In fragrance all things fume,
To all who breathe, recalling
Some sensual indiscretion.
The fireflies light the gloom,
And moist, warm Earth seems falling
For masculine possession.

The waterwheel is hushed,
But murmuring onwards still,
Through ruts and rills afar,
In light, soft whispers rushed,
Reflecting water thrills
To each unfeeling star.

★

Fado-Canção—José Régio

I meditate my own strange lot.
I sing, and know the reason for it.
I sing because I have no better
Gift than this of song.
I sing to fortify myself
Against the silence, and the emptiness
Of my frustrated life,
Against the chill
Which percolates my being—
Like someone who, when night has fallen,
Has got to pass the cross-roads,
And lifts his trembling voice in song
To drive away his terror . . .
Behind the melody,
Which almost seems to speak,
A tragic statue stands in silence.
But sweet the rhythm is that lulls one,
And sweet the rhyme that lures one on,
And so I sing because it eases me
To listen to myself, although
The statue, as in granite, stands
Fixing its eyes afar,
And lifts a finger to its lips
Which stifles and prevents,
Upon those lips that frame a cry,
The cry from being uttered . . .

I also sing because I know
My song does not express me.
No one will ever find more in it
Than play of rhyme or rhythm.
I know quite well, that right up there,
And right down here below
I suffer all alone, hovering in silence—
But yet I sing, to leave
An echo thrilling in the air
Of the futile lullaby
That the sleeping world enjoys.

Ah! There are things that few men know!
But I know
So profoundly!
Those few men, yes, perhaps, may know them,
But cannot feel them truly.
I sing them, and it's plain
That none can recognise them
In the alien tone I give them.
I can never arrive in their midst,
Even when it appears
That, escaping from my own enchantment,
I find myself with my own set of people.
I know all that—I know it well.
I know much more—But still, I sing.

Yes, I sing.
It is my destiny.
But I sing as a child screams
Who clings to the balcony
Of a building that's on fire,
In which he is left forgotten . . .
The square, beneath, is empty.
The sky, above, is hidden.
The balcony is dizzily high;
The ladders are turned to dust and ashes.
The crazy floor is crumbling.
The scream of anguish alone
Pierces an echo in the distance . . .
And no-one comes to his rescue.

I know that no-one is coming,
No-one at all.
The solitude, of which I'm dying,
Lends me a helping hand,
And exchanges a look of kindness
Which saves me from my panic . . .
But how much the better I know
And how much more devoutly believe in
That echo that sounds in the distance . . .

So the louder and better I sing!

★

Counsel—Manuel Bandeira

The world is pitiless and lewdly jeers
All tragedy. Anticipate your loss.
Weep silently, in secret. Hide your tears,
So to become accustomed to your cross.

Alone grief can ennoble us. She only
Is grand and pure. Then learn to love her now—
To be your muse, when you are left and lonely,
And lay the last green laurels on your brow.

She will be sent from Heaven. The seraphic
Language she speaks in, you should learn, for she
Can talk no other in your daily traffic,

When you receive her to replace your bride.
Pray humbly, too, to God, that she may be
A constant, kind companion at your side.